PLAYING IN TRAFFIC ON MADISON AVENUE

TALES OF ADVERTISING'S GLORY YEARS

PLAYING IN TRAFFIC ON MADISON AVENUE
TALES OF ADVERTISING'S GLORY YEARS

David Herzbrun

Dow Jones-Irwin
Homewood, Illinois 60430

Sponsoring editor: Susan Glinert Stevens, Ph.D.
Project editor: Jane Lightell
Production manager: Diane Palmer
Jacket design: Michael Finkelman
Compositor: Eastern Graphics
Typeface: 11/13 Century Schoolbook
Printer: Arcata Graphics/Kingsport

Library of Congress Cataloging-in-Publication Data

Herzbrun, David.
  Playing in traffic on Madison Avenue : tales of advertising's glory years / David Herzbrun.
    p.   cm.
  ISBN 1-55623-338-8
  1. Herzbrun, David. 2. Copy writers—New York (N.Y.)—Biography.
3. Copy writers—New York (N.Y.)—Anecdotes. 4. Advertising—New York (N.Y.)—History. I. Title.
  HD8039.C6542U64   1990
  659.13'2'097471—dc20   89–48445
                                                        CIP

Printed in the United States of America
1 2 3 4 5 6 7 8 9 0 K 7 6 5 4 3 2 1 0

For Ellen,
who was with me every step
and misstep of the way and
who has no need to read this.

CONTENTS

THE FUTURE IS MERCHANDISING, 1

SO THIS IS ADVERTISING, 13

SUKIE AND THE GOLD MINE, 20

A PERFORMING ART, 24

MORE STEPPING STONES, 40

THE INNER SANCTUM, 54

INNOCENTS ABROAD, 71

PUTTING MY BOOK TOGETHER, 103

CONFESSIONS OF AN OGILVY MAN, 113

THE ART OF THE POSSIBLE, 134

TRAVELING ON, 160

TRAVELING FURTHER ON, 165

MY NAME ON A DOOR, 168

BETWEEN ROLES, 173

IN THE TIME MACHINE, 178

AIN'T IT HELL? 193

INTERLUDE, WITH MBAs, 204

ON THE ROAD AGAIN, 208

LAST AGENCY BEFORE THE TURNPIKE, 221

THE FUTURE IS
MERCHANDISING

In my senior year at Marlboro College, a tiny school in southern Vermont, Dean Roland Boyden advised me to become a copywriter.

I had asked for his advice and his help in getting a job as a teacher of literature at some university, which I thought would be a good way to support my habit of writing poetry.

"I think teaching wouldn't be the best career choice for you," he said. "You are a quick student, but you're not a scholar. You have a great deal of breadth, but very little depth. Your best gift is . . . glibness? Let's call it verbal dexterity. Have you thought about going into advertising?"

The competition was fierce.

I was part of what Life magazine called "the biggest graduating class in history," meaning all the graduates of all the colleges and universities in the country. It was 1950, and we were the first four-year postwar class.

Most of us, myself included, were veterans. We were a self-confident, ambitious lot with rich and varied life experiences not commonly found in damp, new graduates. Some of us still thought of ourselves as kids, but others had already held command positions and were very grown up. One of my classmates had been a major in an infantry regiment in Europe. And outside of my own little college class—seven of us received degrees—there were tens of thousands of tough, smart, impressive

1

young men mailing out resumes, looking for challenging career opportunities.

I was competing against them for a job in an ad agency mailroom.

There were no training programs in agencies in those days, and the mailroom was where you started if you wanted to be a copywriter or an account executive.

If you wanted to be a layout man (art directors hadn't been invented yet), you got a job in the bullpen cutting type apart with razor blades and pasting up mechanicals. Layout men didn't have to go through the mailroom experience, but they had already learned a trade in a commercial art school—not that it would help them in the long run, because layout men never got anywhere. Who ever heard of an ad agency with a layout man's name on the door?

It didn't take long for me to find out that every mailroom on Madison Avenue was already fully staffed with tall, handsome Ivy League graduates who had been air force colonels. When I showed up, not tall and handsome, vaguely Jewish, from an unknown college I had helped found just three years earlier, and with discharge papers from the merchant marine, personnel directors did all but snicker.

I needed connections.

My father had one friend in advertising, a man named Sam Cher, who was Vice President in charge of something or other at Young & Rubicam.

"I could get you a job in the mailroom," he said, "but I don't want to see you start out that way. I want to see you come into this business with some special skill or knowledge that will separate you from the herd and put you out ahead. Now, these days a lot of smart people believe the future of advertising is merchandising. That'll be the magic word in two or three years. You take a year or two to learn merchandising, and there'll be no stopping you. That's my advice."

I asked him what merchandising was.

"Well, I'm no expert," he said, "but I believe the best place to learn about it—to learn what makes people buy and how they act when they interact with merchandise in a store—is in a store. You should get into one of those training programs they have at Macy's or Gimbels. Do that, and come back and see me in a year or two."

It took another of my father's connections, plus some fast talking on my part, to get accepted by Gimbels's Executive Training Squad.

The Squad was made up of twenty young men (women, like art directors, hadn't been invented yet), recruited from the best colleges and screened from over five hundred applicants. The pay was $40 a week, which gave me a take-home of $27 and change.

Inevitably, most of the Squad's members were veterans. Some were tough, wised-up, worldly guys of my age, 23, while others were cynical, hard-bitten, craggy-faced bourbon drinkers of 27.

The Squad was fired by a collective will to win, and they hit the Basement running.

Notice that *they*. Personally, I hit the Basement cringing. I hated the store on sight, and the Basement, where we all started out learning as sales clerks, seemed to me to have been designed by Dante. Our customers were Daumier drawings. And the place smelled funny.

I served my time in the Basement, learning how to write up sales in a salesbook with four interleaved carbons and how to use a cash register.

I also learned a curious thing about the way people buy, and I think it embodied a principle that I later learned to use in making advertising. It was this: I was kept busy by a mob of women madly buying long underwear, which was tangled like snakes in a pit, in an open bin. They weren't sorted by sizes, and the women were busily searching for what they wanted, snatching underwear out of each other's hands and bickering like sparrows. When things slowed down a little, I took the occasion to sort the underwear by size and to fold it neatly. And that's when the action stopped, with hardly a sale for the rest of the day.

The next morning was pretty slow at the long-johns counter, and I got a hunch. I messed everything up. Sure enough, the things looked like bargains again, and again I was surrounded by shoppers.

Maybe this was merchandising.

Maybe it was just the same principle that Robert Herrick wrote about in "Delight in Disorder":

> A winning wave, deserving note,
> In the tempestuous petticoat,
> A careless shoestring, in whose tie
> I see a wild civility,
> Do more bewitch me than when art
> Is too precise in every part

Years later, I learned to put it this way: The best advertising looks as if it had been made by human hands.

But I was still a long way from advertising. First I had to work my way through Receiving and Marking, Haberdashery, Kitchenware and Small Appliances, Auditing, and Leather Goods.

Nowhere did I hear a word about Merchandising, only about merchandise.

Our Personnel Director, a nice man named Ellis Greenfield, saw that I was unhappy. (I had managed to conceal from him that I was, in fact, miserable and that I did not seem to share the Squad's killer instinct.) When he discussed it with me, I confessed that retailing was not to be my life's work, and I hadn't the "calling" but was only using it as a way station on the path to copywriting. He was sympathetic.

"Of course I can't put you in the Advertising Department," he said.

"Of course," I agreed. It was well known that Bernice Fitz-Gibbon, the fabled lady who ran Gimbels's advertising, would hire no copywriter who was not a member of Phi Beta Kappa. I have never understood this, but then again, I have never understood why her most famous slogan, "Nobody but nobody undersells Gimbels," was any good.

"I knew you'd understand," Greenfield said. "However, if you want to write for a living, I do have an opening. The editor of *The Gimbelite* has just resigned, and we need someone to take over. It requires a knowledge of the store, a better than nodding acquaintance with all departments, and we've certainly trained you for that. And if you can write clearly, lay out a paper, and get it printed, it just might be a good spot for you. Can you handle it?"

Handle it? It was made for me! With my experience on the high school and college papers, it would be a snap.

I told him this and added that I had studied illustration, could do cartoons and caricatures, could take pictures and specify type. I would be *The Gimbelite*'s Harold Ross and would transform it into *The New Yorker* of house organs.

Well, it wasn't a bad job. I had an office of my own, which is a rarity for all but the top management in any big store. I made my own hours. I collected the news (weddings, births, anniversaries, promotions, deaths) from departmental stringers, and I wrote up the stories for them I wrote feature articles, light verse, and editorials. I drew cartoons, specified type, pasted up the page layouts, and worked with the printer, a generous man who took the time to tour me through his plant and teach me what I had to know about production. If the result looked a little like a high school paper, what else could be expected?

I did a series of interviews with top executives, many of them Merchandise Managers. I asked each one about Merchandising, and mostly they connected it with either buying or displaying goods. None of them had any idea of how it might be applied to advertising.

I finally figured that I knew as much about Merchandising as I was going to learn at Gimbels. I had been there for two years, was earning $60 a week, and felt that I was ready to go back to Sam Cher.

Again he saw me because of my father. I'm pretty sure he didn't remember seeing me two years before. I told him what I had been up to and asked if he could help me get started in advertising.

He told me that all he could do was get me a job in the mailroom at $40 a week, but he would hate to see me take a step backward like that. I had a wife and a baby by then, and I hated the idea of a cut even more than he did.

"Too bad," Cher added, "that you spent two important early years on the wrong track. But I'm sure you can get a job writing copy in Gimbels's Ad Department, and a few years of that will set you straight."

I didn't have a chance to tell him about the Phi Beta Kappa policy because by then we were on a down elevator and he said his last few words to me as he was getting out. He gave me a cheery wave as the doors shut, and I went down and out to the unwelcoming pavement of Madison Avenue.

The man had wasted two years of my life and had never noticed it.

But of course nothing is ever really wasted.

I had my bundle of *Gimbelites* to show that I could write, and while ad agency Copy Chiefs (creative directors hadn't been invented yet) would refuse to even look at them, I knew they would help me get some sort of job.

The job was another house organ editing job, this time for Executone, a company that made intercom systems. I didn't want to be editor of the *Executone News*, but I wanted the job because the title wasn't Editor, but Copywriter in the Advertising Department. I was even promised a chance to write some advertising, if I was a good boy.

The job consisted largely of reading sales reports in hopes of finding some unusual and interesting use for an intercom system. When I found a good story, I would write it up so that salesmen would read it and get inspired with a new selling idea. If, for example, I noticed that an Executone System had been sold to a car wash in Minneapolis, I was supposed to wonder what in hell a car wash would do with an intercom and then find out about it. If they had a good use for one that would apply to other car washes, the *Executone News* had a useful, lead-generating story.

What I did instead, most of the time, was pick up on strange company names and track them down to see if there were good stories behind them. What was the Oriental Show-You in Nutley, New Jersey? How did they use an intercom system? What was the Better Monkey Grip Company? What was a monkey grip? I found this sort of thing endlessly fascinating.

I never did get a story by following up on weird company names. What I usually got was a disappointment, such as discovering that the Ten Mile Collision Company in Detroit was not commemorating some monumental crack-up, but was merely located on Ten Mile Road. Or discovering that the Purefag Hotel in Talladega, Florida, was actually the Purefoy.

Between these feckless forays into investigative journalism, I actually managed to get out a few issues of the *Executone News*, despite the fact that I was also writing the lyrics to an off-Broadway musical comedy at the time. In the office.

It's a tribute to the patience of my boss, Herb Federbush, that he took nine months of this before he fired me. He said, "You're talented, I think, but probably not as a copywriter. I think you ought to find another line of work."

And it's a tribute to Herb's graciousness that he phoned me years later to congratulate me on becoming Creative Director at Ogilvy & Mather and reminded me of what he had said when he had fired me.

I told him that he had been right.

Walter Lowen ran the big advertising placement service in New York. (Headhunters hadn't been invented yet.) I went there, filled out some job application forms, and wasn't interviewed. A secretary told me that Mr. Lowen or one of his associates would get in touch with me when something opened up, but not to hold my breath.

Jerry Fields ran the only other game in town. His new, little company wasn't even in an office building like Walter Lowen's but in a store, two steps down from the street, in the West 40s. It didn't look like an office either. It had exposed brick walls, some palms and ferns, and old stripped oak furniture bleached to a pale bone color. There were some posters on the walls and some framed turn-of-the-century ads.

Thousands of restaurants and bars look like that today, but I had never seen anything like it then. It was light and bright and young, and it gave me the feeling that advertising just might be a creative business, a place for smart young people, a lively and inventive environment. It's odd that Jerry's low budget, makeshift, decor gave me the first glimmering of what was to come.

But it wasn't to come just yet.

Jerry interviewed me and even gave me a cup of coffee, but with very little encouragement to sweeten it.

"You're not ready," he told me. "No ad agency would hire you based on stuff like that. But I have got one slightly wild idea that might be worth looking into."

The slightly wild idea was a job writing catalog copy for Sears Roebuck & Company. I had never heard anything less wild and few things more dismal. On the other hand, I had just been fired and had a wife and a baby to feed.

Jerry made it worse. "You'd have to move to Chicago if you got the job, but it would only be for a couple of years. Then they'd move you to someplace else. Not New York."

Then he made it even worse. "They're using some kind of battery of psychological tests to screen applicants. It takes two days to take the tests. They have three job openings, and they're testing four or five hundred people. They said they have all the applicants they need now, but I think I could talk them into testing one more. Interested?"

I was only interested to know how psychological testing could help Sears screen for potential catalog copywriters, but Jerry didn't know. I said I would do it anyway, because I had no other leads at all. Jerry called and set it up and told me to show up at Sears's New York offices in two days.

I spent the next two days answering want ads.

One little ray of hope appeared at an otherwise hopeless ad agency called Gasman & Levin. Arthur Gasman, President of this gloomy, shabby, Dickensian establishment, wanted an assistant. It would be a chance to learn the agency business, write copy, do some account management, plan media, and do all the little things, like sales promotion, that a small ad agency gets involved in.

Of course I would have taken it in an instant, Sears be damned, but Arthur Gasman didn't offer it. He had a couple of other applicants to see, but he made nice, encouraging noises and assured me that he'd get back to me in a week.

At Sears the next day, a personnel man explained the tests. "We ran psychological profiles on a number of our most successful executives," he told me, showing me an example of a psychological profile. It looked like a drawing of a mountain range.

"We found that the profiles of our best managers were remarkably similar," he went on. "Then we made a composite profile to use as a sort of template. This is it." It looked a lot like the other mountain range.

He told me that if my profile came close to that of the template, and if I scored high enough on the IQ test and the general achievement test, it would demonstrate that I would be a Sears executive personality, bound to succeed in the firm.

Then he outlined the future, year for year, for, the decade to come. It was minutely programmed. It posited my salary for each year, in constant dollars, and it ended with a vision of me as a Merchandising (?) Manager earning $40,000 a year in 1962.

The number was awe-inspiring but not unimaginable. I didn't have to imagine it because I had once met a man who earned $40,000 a year. He told me so while we sat on the porch of his house in Connecticut looking over his swimming pool and tennis court, his paddock and his horses.

A tempting vision to be sure, but I was not tempted by what I would have to do and be to get there via Sears. In fact, I was more than a little frightened and very uncomfortable in the presence of this huge, omniscient organization that had the ability to see ten years into the future and that had the means to probe the minds and hearts of young applicants, to gather unto its bosom its own, for purposes of its own.

I decided that nothing could ever make me work for Sears Roebuck & Company.

Despite this, I did take the tests. It was one way to kill two days, waiting for Arthur Gasman to hire me.

My approach to the tests was to ask myself how a successful Sears executive would answer the questions. I took a few minutes to imagine such a man. His name was Francis, but he called himself Pete. He was in his early thirties, was earning forty grand, had worked in stores in Kansas City, Seattle, and Atlanta and was now back home in Chicago, living in Lake Forest.

I set about the test in a novelist's frame of mind, letting the questions clarify and define Pete's personality.

The questions were mostly multiple choice. One that I remember clearly—it might have been the first one—was this:

> You have unexpectedly been given a day off. What would you most like to do?
> 1. Go to a baseball game.
> 2. Play golf.
> 3. Read a novel.
> 4. Go fishing.

Well, "read a novel" was an obvious loser. The tipoff was *novel*, which called up an image of the epicene young executive coyly reclining on a chaise longue and nibbling bonbons. But what could be wrong with the other choices?

The way I worked it out, going to a ball game, however all-American, was passive, not participatory, and that sure didn't sound like Pete. Fishing was solitary, maybe even antisocial, and even if Pete liked to fish, he would be too smart to say so. That left golf as the clear winner. It was participatory, it was sociable, it could be combined with business, and it had just enough snob appeal.

Before the two days were over, I had come to deeply dislike Francis "Pete" Mills. He had earned his last name because "the mills of God grind slowly yet they grind exceeding small."

I disliked Pete, but I knew that I had got him right. As the hours wore on, each question seemed to summon him up, like some imp from hell answering a cabalistic chant. I finished the tests on Friday afternoon, went home and whined to Ellen about what the world was coming to. It wouldn't be the last time.

On Tuesday Arthur Gasman offered me the job, starting at $85 a week with a $15 raise in three months if I worked out well. I thanked him politely and accepted, after I had finished sobbing and kissing the hem of his garment.

I was to start the following Monday, picking up neatly just as my two weeks' severance from Executone was used up.

The next day I got a call from Sears. In hushed tones, the personnel man told me that I was one of the three testees selected for anointment. I told him I wasn't interested, but thanks anyway.

"No, no, you don't understand," he said. "They're coming in to see you on Friday. Three of our very top men. They're really excited. You have to be here."

I assured him that nothing would make me work for Sears.

"But that can't be," he said in a panicky voice. "The tests prove that you're a Sears success story. You couldn't be happy working anywhere else."

I told him I had cheated on the tests.

"Everyone cheats. The tests adjust for that. The men whose profiles were used to create the composite template probably cheated too, but the people who designed the tests accounted for all that. They figure that if you cheated the same way the role models did, then you're actually one of them."

I tried to imagine Francis "Pete" Mills, in real life, actually using the day he had designated for golf to sneak off and read a novel, but I just couldn't do it.

I failed to convince the personnel man that a career at Sears was the single worst idea I had ever heard. He wore me down with his refusal to believe anything but the infallibility of the tests. Finally, I agreed, reluctantly, to come in on Friday to meet the men from Chicago, "just for the sake of courtesy." I knew, and he knew that I knew, that he just didn't want the job of explaining my decision to them, and since he had done nothing to deserve that job, I agreed to do it myself.

On Friday, after a fifteen minute wait in the reception room reading a Sears Annual Report that convinced me that Sears was pretty damn big and made a whole lot of money, I was led into a huge conference room. At the far end of a long, long table, three men rose as I entered. They were big, solid-looking men who looked as if they belonged in rooms like this one. I suddenly felt very small, frail, and young—too small and frail to cross the vast distance of that room, hampered as I was by carpeting with ankle-deep velvety pile. I struggled and waded through it toward the distant voices of the men rumbling deep-throated, sincere words of praise and welcome. I stopped a yard or two short of them. I didn't want to get close enough for handshakes; I was afraid they would never let go.

"I only came to tell you I've accepted another job," I croaked.

"If you have, it was a mistake," one of them said.

"You can tell them you got the offer you've always been waiting for," said another.

"We're not surprised you've had another offer," the third said. "Minds like yours are in great demand, always were, always will be. Look, you can call them from here, give them your regrets."

It took a while to convince them that I was really not going to work for Sears. That was hard enough, but it was impossible to make them understand why a job at a little agency called Gasman & Levin was more attractive to me, and equally impossible to make them believe that I was not one of them but an imposter who had fooled the test makers.

They continued to try to talk me into taking the job as I backed my way to the door, stumbling through the carpet, gabbling thanks, farewells, and apologies all at once.

I was leaving the world of programmed, assured success for the sure uncertainties of advertising, and I was filled with elation.

SO THIS IS ADVERTISING

Gasman & Levin occupied a small suite of rooms at the top of a shabby little office building on the corner of 46th Street and 6th Avenue. (The Avenue of the Americas hadn't been invented yet.)

Behind a sort of teller's window in the miniature reception room sat Jean Katz, receptionist, secretary, bookkeeper, and switchboard operator. Past her room, in the corner office, Arthur Gasman sat with his back to the sunlight that made his jug-handle ears a luminescent pink. "Welcome aboard," he said cheerily. "I'll see you in a few minutes."

Jean took me to the office next to Arthur's. It belonged to Murray Levin, who was packing up his things to clear it out. "Arthur's a wonderful man," he told me. "We had a very good partnership, but it's time for me to move on to other things. I guess you'll have this office. Good luck in it."

Next down the line was a man named Byron Something who was in charge of production, but he also wrote copy and did some media planning. And past his office, at the end of the short corridor, was the Art Department, where three grey-faced middle-aged men sat hunched over drawing boards working at a slow, steady pace to the sound of classical music from a cheap, tinny radio.

For the first few days, while Murray Levin completed his packing, I sat next to Arthur Gasman's desk and watched everything he did. He wrote copy, did rough layouts, worked out media plans (I looked up circulations and rates of publications for him in *Standard Rate & Data* while he wrote down the information), and between all this he dealt with clients on the telephone.

We (he) did ads for British Industries' products, all of them

13

in the brand-new field of high fidelity sound components. People in the know were just beginning to say *hi fi*, and only a few on the leading edge of technology knew of the existence of what was called *binaural sound*, which we now call stereo.

Our products were Garrard Record Changers (turntables hadn't been invented yet), Leak amplifiers, Wharfedale speakers, Multicore Solder and KT-66 tubes. (This was before solid state, too.)

I discovered to my horror that Arthur had hired me because I had been a supposed copywriter at Executone and must therefore know all about electronics. The fact was that it had never even occurred to me that an intercom system was an electronic device. I'm pretty sure, too, that I could not have defined *electronic* or said how it differed from *electrical*. And all my years in school and college had taught me to hate and fear anything technical or scientific.

I didn't know anything at all about electronics. But I knew how to read. So I read every ad Arthur had written in the last three years, and when I finally had to do my first ad, a one-third pager for Garrard, I parroted what I had read. Arthur thought I was a genius.

I moved into Murray Levin's office, a small room with a one-window view south over 46th Street, and dug into writing copy, sketching out rough layouts, and checking type proofs. I wrote electronics ads, of course, but I also had a chance to work on other things. I wrote ads for a cemetery in New Jersey, a power lawn mower, an audio store called Sun Radio, and Zyl Plastic, which was used to make eyeglass frames.

After a month of turning out ads, Arthur called me in for a talk.

"You're doing a great job," he said, "and I don't want to keep you waiting another two months to raise you to $100. It'll be in your next paycheck. And, by the way, Byron is leaving us, and until I can find a replacement for him, I'd like you to take over his work. Okay?"

Of course it was okay. Anything Arthur wanted was okay for $100 a week. That was more than $5,000 a year! Easy Street was just a few short blocks away.

Of course, doing Byron's job as well as mine meant longer

hours, but that was okay too. It was only until Arthur could find a replacement for Byron. But after a few weeks it became clear that he wasn't looking for one, and I still didn't feel quite secure enough to complain about it. Besides, I was learning about production, and I liked it. Our typographer, our engraver, and our printer all took me on tours of their plants and explained the different steps. They taught me to appreciate good work and to spot bad work. Pretty soon I understood what it was that I was buying, found that the more I knew the less time the job took, and began to relax into an easier schedule.

Then the Art Department quit.

Arthur explained to me that it really wasn't his Art Department at all, but an independent studio that he had made a deal with, exchanging space for work. It was a fairly commonplace way to do business, he said, and he would just have to find a new studio operator to move in. Until then, I would act as Art Buyer. It would probably take me no more than a couple of extra hours a week, but it wouldn't be long until he got a new studio in, and anyway he'd make it up to me when my six-month review came around, okay?

Sure it was okay.

I talked to Kurt, who headed the studio, and asked him what an Art Buyer did and how to do it. He suggested a few free lancers I could call to do mechanicals, told me about the Society of Illustrators, and put me on to the few publications that showcased the work of commercial photographers.

I started buying art. I never had much money to spend, so I had to give most of the work to young people who were just getting a start. One who I used just once (when I called him the second time he had raised his prices out of our range) was a new kid named Andy Warhol. I had him draw a trolley car. He said he wasn't sure he could do a good trolley car because all he'd been doing was drawing women's shoes, but he'd be glad to try. I remember it was a swell trolley car.

Most of the work wasn't this creative, and all of it was done under terrific time pressure and for the cheapest possible prices. One of the worst jobs came up every quarter—a catalog we had to turn out for a client who made baby hats. About sixty different hats were in that catalog, and we had to use at least thirty different babies as models because after the second shot the kids usually started howling. I was at the shoot—the first shoot I ever covered—and we actually got through the whole thing in two days. That means we spent about ten minutes on each hat, which didn't leave much time for subtleties of lighting or for conning the babies into looking, if not happy, at least out of pain. For the entire two days there was a constant noise of babies screaming and mothers talking above the sound. The place looked and sounded like what Ellis Island must have been in the 1880s.

The resulting catalog—a collection of black and white photos of sullen babies, babies on the brink of tears, and babies just recovering from a good cry—was as depressing a piece of advertising literature as I have since seen, but the client loved it. The photographer, an old hand at this sort of thing, had set up the lighting so that the hats would show up in complete, if inartistic, detail. He made no concession as to how the kids would look. Of course the manufacturer looked only at his hats and congratulated me for doing a wonderful job of art direction.

I was writing a zingy, expressive, witty, and motivating piece of copy for Multicore Solder when Arthur came into my office and sat down.

"You're doing a great job," he said.

"Which one? Copywriter? Production Man? Art Buyer? Layout Man?"

"Don't worry," he said, "we'll get some help soon. But what I want to talk to you about now is whether you think you can take over my job for a week."

He explained that he hadn't had a vacation in years because he hadn't felt that he could trust anyone to look after the agency. (What had Murray Levin's job been?) Nowadays, with me looking after so much of the work anyway, he felt confident that he could leave for a week, provided I was not worried about it.

I told him that I was sure I could do it for a week, as long as he would give me a complete list of what needed doing. Arthur was so happy that he gave me a ten buck raise effective immediately. A few days later, he took his wife to Florida.

The week went easily, and it was kind of fun. I enjoyed calling on British Industries out on Long Island, and even driving to the cemetery in New Jersey to present work. Toward the end of the week I went downtown to visit Sun Radio and get instructions on a new campaign they wanted, and I took the advertising manager to lunch. A first. He ordered a martini, and so did I. Another first. And a second.

I was feeling wonderful that afternoon when Arthur phoned. I told him expansively that I had made it through the week without a hitch and that everything was in great shape, just great. He was delighted to hear that, he said, because if it was okay with me he wanted to stay on in Florida for another week's vacation.

"Of course, of course, have a wonderful, wonderful time," the martini said.

It wasn't until later that evening that the fear set in. I had no list of instructions for the second week. Sun wanted to see a new campaign theme, with layouts and copy, by Thursday. British Industries wanted a revised media plan for Garrard and also asked for a meeting on Tuesday to demonstrate some new models of Wharfedale speakers and get us started on ads and brochures for them. I knew I was in over my head.

On Monday morning I got in early, and as soon as Jean came in I had her phone Arthur. He had checked out of his hotel and left no forwarding address. My heart sank.

I started to work up the Sun Radio campaign, and with the help of Kurt, our ex-studio head, got a pretty good thing going. I got through the Garrard media meeting with a plan that Jean worked up. It wasn't right, but the client enjoyed telling me how wrong it was and making all the necessary changes. I handled the Wharfedale meeting by listening to the new speakers with an expression of rapt enchantment, keeping my mouth shut, and taking lots of notes. I began to think I was going to get through the week alive.

On Thursday morning, as I was putting the Sun campaign layouts and copy into a portfolio, Jean came in to see me. She said, "Don't let them keep any of that material unless you get a check for $4,000. They're way behind on their payments."

I told her I wasn't sure I could pull it off. I had never tried to be, or even to act like a bill collector, and I was afraid they wouldn't take me seriously.

"You better make them take you seriously," she said, "because this is serious. We're just about out of money in the regular agency account. I can pay our salaries tomorrow, but there's not enough there for me to pay the rent next week. Of course Mr. Gasman will be back next week and he'll know what to do, but all the same . . . ."

The Sun Ad Manager liked the campaign, but when I asked him for the money he brushed the request aside. He said he had approved the invoice a few days ago and had sent it along to accounting. I asked him if he could call accounting and get them to bring in a check while I waited, and he said that was out of the question, that it would just have to go through the pipeline in the regular way. We would surely have it next week.

I didn't see that there was any reasonable answer to that, so I just thanked him for his approval of the campaign and went back to tell Jean about the money.

"Oh, God, that's what he's been saying for the last two months. I wish Mr. Gasman would call!"

He called late that afternoon, was delighted to hear that Sun had bought the campaign, authorized another ten buck raise for me as soon as he got back, and said, "I'll call you next week about the same time Thursday or Friday."

"Wait!" I yelled into a disconnected line.

Ellen and I lived in Riverdale in the Bronx, and I commuted by train to Grand Central. I rode in every day with a graphic designer named Aaron Burns and his wife Florence.

During the next week, the third week of Arthur's vacation, Florence commented that I was looking kind of jumpy and unhappy, so I told them what had been going on.

"Quit," Aaron said lightly and cheerfully. "You shouldn't have to put up with all that for a lousy salary."

I explained how long it had taken and how hard it had been for me to find a job as a copywriter, no matter how lousy it was, and that I didn't think it would be a whole lot easier with only six months of experience behind me and a generally undistinguished book of samples.

Aaron told me I could always free lance and that I would probably make more money at it and certainly have more fun and freedom. I had done a couple of free-lance jobs with him in the last few months, giving me the only good samples I had, and Aaron said there was a lot of good work to be had "out there."

We talked about it all week on the train. Aaron promised to introduce me to all the right people, the new wave of graphic designers who needed a copywriter who understood visual thinking. The names meant nothing to me: Lou Dorfsman, Herb Lubalin, Bill Golden, Bob Gill, Ivan Chermayoff, Saul Bass, Herb Roan, Ariosto Nardozzi. Aaron made them sound like a very exciting bunch.

When Arthur returned, I gave him two weeks' notice and explained what I wanted to do. He offered to help with introductions and references.

He resigned the Sun Radio account and recommended that I do their work on a free-lance basis. They agreed, and I made a deal that included payment for each job 50 percent up front. It wasn't much, but it was a start.

Sun was the only piece of business I was able to pick up when Arthur resigned every account but British Industries, which he joined as Advertising Manager, taking Jean Katz with him. He was really relieved that I had quit, so much so that he found the money to pay my back salary plus the two weeks I had given him as notice.

SUKIE AND THE GOLD MINE

My father let me use a desk, a typewriter, and a file cabinet in his office at 1440 Broadway in the Garment District. I had letterheads and business cards printed that read "Copy Associates" with my name centered below. I had figured that I might be able to overcome my lack of experience by pretending that I was representing a string of experienced copywriters, all employed at major agencies, who were available for moonlighting assignments. No matter what the assignment, I would find one who had a terrific background in the category.

Armed with the cheap card and this flimsy lie, I answered every ad in the *Times*. I struck gold when I met Jack Danowitz at Florida Fashions.

Jack was Advertising Manager of this mail order dress business. They had no retail outlets at all and existed solely on advertising. Nobody I knew had ever heard of them, yet their major annual catalogs had a mailed distribution of five million copies, about the circulation of *Life* magazine at the time.

Florida Fashions customers were mostly farm women, or at least women who lived in rural areas or very small towns. They bought dresses by mail order because there was no other way to buy them in towns like Opp, Alabama, unless you wanted to take the bus thirty miles to Dothan.

Jack Danowitz said that he'd be happy to try out one of my mythical string of mail-order dress-catalog specialists. He would pay $15 for a catalog page, no matter what the page included. One page could be devoted to a single featured garment, such as a lace-trimmed dark velvet dress with a neckline that converted from high-buttoned modesty, suitable for funerals, to a low-plunging come-on that would light up any farm lady's fantasies. A page like that, at $15, was a rare gift for a copywriter.

The more typical Florida Fashions page had as many as eighteen different house dresses pictured, each of which had to be sold hard in a couple of sentences and detailed in matters of available sizes and colors. All that for the same $15.

I quickly calculated that if I could get to write seven pages a week, I'd just about equal my Gasman & Levin pay and still have time to do some work for Sun Radio on the side. I told Jack that I'd like to try doing it myself, and he said he was willing to pay me for a trial run. He gave me a catalog to study plus pictures and fact sheets on ten dresses that would be shown on the page.

I hurried back to my father's office, studied the catalog for a while, and knocked out a headline I thought was in their style. It was something like "Picture yourself in picture-pretty prints!" and was followed by a short paragraph about spring fashions. I then whizzed through the ten dress descriptions, "wide-swinging nine-gore skirt" and so forth, and rushed back to show the work to Jack.

He said he hadn't expected to see me for a couple of days, and then he read every word, slowly and carefully, with a critical scowl.

"Not bad," he said at last. "Some of it's a little clever—we don't want clever, we want clear—but you got the idea all right. You want to do three more pages?"

I had the three pages finished before lunch the next day, but decided to wait till nearly 5 o'clock to deliver them. I didn't want Jack to think it was too easy for me.

He told me he hadn't expected to see me for a couple of more days. He read carefully, as before, holding a blue pencil poised above the copy. He made a few changes and handed the copy back to me.

"I just cut out some clever you sneaked in," he said. "I also changed some words our readers maybe wouldn't understand." He paused for a moment and cleared his throat before teaching me one of the most important lessons I was ever to learn as a copywriter.

"You got to remember," he said, "our ladies are mostly not

very educated, but that doesn't mean they're dumb. I figure intelligence happens about as often among the poor as it does among the rich, the same with those who went to college and the ones never graduated grade school. Now, you take a badly educated intelligent lady and give her a word she don't understand and you make her feel dumb and that makes her feel bad, and when she feels bad, she's not in a buying mood. You make her feel dumb a couple of times, she won't read your catalog again; she'll buy dresses from somebody makes her feel smart."

He assigned me three more pages.

I knew I would write them all the next day, and I would make my goal for the week, seven pages for $105. And the next day was only Wednesday!

For the next three and a half weeks, I wrote every single page Jack had to offer, and when the month was finished, I had done sixty pages and had earned $900. That was more than twice what Arthur had paid me, and the work had only taken about half my time. Visions of Connecticut horse farms danced in my head.

Jack told me that he was starting to put together one of Florida Fashions' two major annual catalogs and that the work load would be heavy and steady. He suggested that I could probably turn out more work with less effort if I stopped running back and forth between my office at 1440 Broadway and his place, some five blocks away. He offered me an office rent free, plus free secretarial help and phone, if I'd move in with him. This also would give me the advantage of seeing the dresses themselves instead of pictures and descriptions. I agreed, and Jack said he'd have a room fixed up for me in a week.

When I came to move in, Jack showed me my new quarters with a gesture of pride. I had never before seen anything like that room. It was a windowless space about 25 feet long and about 6 feet wide. At the far end of this cavern stood a desk with its typing return facing the doorway. Suspended from the ceiling, a garment rack like the ones used by dry cleaners ran from one side of the doorway to the desk, made a U-turn in front of the typewriter, and ran back to the other side of the doorway.

Jack showed me how the garment rack worked. A stock boy would bring in dresses and hang them on the right hand side. I would pull a sort of drapery cord, and the dresses would come down the line one at a time to hang in front of the typewriter. I could look at them, feel them, read the information tags, and type away. While reading what I had written, I would be able to pull the cord and deliver the next dress while the previous one started its trip up the return rail to the doorway.

Jack left. I sat in the typist's chair and watched while a stock boy hung a batch of dresses on the rack and handed me a tally sheet that told me which stock numbers were to be grouped on a page. I reeled in a dress, put a sheet of paper in the typewriter, and started reading the hang tag. Jack came back into the room.

"Before you get going, I've got something I want you to have," he said. He handed me a framed picture. "I want to have it hung behind your desk so you see her first thing you come in every morning. She's your reader. Her name is Sukie."

Sukie was black, fat, and unappealing. She stared at the camera with an expression of uncomprehending and stolid patience mingled with suspicion and low cunning.

"Don't give me any knee-jerk liberal reactions," Jack said. "This is just one of our customers, and she sent us the picture herself for a prize promotion we did a couple years ago. It wasn't a beauty contest; it was a lottery, so anybody could enter. Sukie is about average. I just want you to have her picture so the next time you try clever or use an unusual word, you can turn around and ask Sukie if she understands."

I can still see Sukie in my mind's eye today as clearly as I saw her every day for the next few months. I never did get used to her. I never got used to the endless parade of dresses that clanked down the rack to my desk. Fortunately, I never got used to the money, either. It came to more than $1,200—that's eighty pages—each month. So when Jerry Fields called to ask me if I'd be interested in a job as merchandising manager at the *American Home* magazine, paying a salary of $150 a week, I told him I would love it.

I did ask him what a Merchandising Manager did for a magazine.

He didn't know and made me promise to tell him when I found out.

A PERFORMING ART

Weldon Willis wasn't too clear about it either, but that didn't stop him from hiring me. My Gimbels training convinced him right away that I knew all about merchandising.

Weldon was new in his job as Sales Promotion manager, a job usually held by a copywriter. Weldon was not a copywriter, but he was married to Jean Austin, the magazine's Food Editor and daughter of Mrs. Austin, the Executive Editor and co-owner of the *American Home*. This was certainly a good background, but it hadn't quite prepared him for creating mailers, promotional packages, and presentations. He assumed that I would do those things, that they were part of merchandising the magazine.

I had no idea of how to go about doing any part of my new job and would never have accepted it if Weldon hadn't been so obviously ignorant about what was expected of me.

So I took it on with one assumption: I would learn how to do the job before he learned that I couldn't do it.

I acted like a Merchandising Manager and Sales Promotion writer while I learned everything I could from an acquaintance at *Collier*'s magazine and a friend of his at *Look*. While I was doing this, everyone at the *American Home* was happy to accept me as a pro.

I think this was my first inkling of what has since become a guiding principle: Life is a performing art.

Years later, Harry Hamburg, a director of commercials, was lunching with me at a Hollywood restaurant where the service was dreadful. Harry complained to the waiter who whined that we had to be patient with him because he wasn't really a waiter but an actor. Harry said to him, "I'm a director, and I can give you some good professional advice. *Act* like a waiter."

Well, I acted like a Sales Promotion man and Merchandising Manager, and Weldon never found out that I was acting. I learned how to do the job, but the most important thing I learned was the principle. It would serve me for the rest of my life in advertising.

It didn't take me very long to learn how to do magazine sales promotion and merchandising, and it didn't take much longer than that to get bored silly doing it.

The job consisted of such things as getting advertisers to take space in a July issue devoted to Family Foods For Fun on the Fourth. For this event, I created a flyer packed in a large red mailing tube with a big fake fuse on one end. The tube was labeled "Explosive Advertising Medium!"

I don't offer this as an example of how terrific I was at this work. I simply want to give you the flavor of what I was doing for a living, and why it didn't take a year before I was back on the phone with Jerry Fields, only this time it was my nickel.

I also called Aaron Burns and asked him to pass the word around that I was looking for a job or even some free-lance work just to keep me from going brain dead. He introduced me to two designers who were to change my life without noticing it while they were changing the look of advertising and graphics around the world. They were Lou Dorfsman, who was Advertising Director of CBS Radio Network, and Herb Lubalin, who headed the Art Department at Sudler & Hennessey, an ethical pharmaceutical agency.

They had no job openings, but they did have some free-lance work. I did a few jobs for each of them, beginning an association that lasted the rest of Herb's life (he died in 1981) and that still goes on with occasional free-lance work with Lou.

I learned from them a new idea in making advertising: that

the visual and the headline, at their ideal best, should do more than go together. They should be inseparable, so that the headline without the visual will be nearly meaningless and the visual without the headline will be at least obscure. This may sound like an obvious idea, or it may sound like an unnecessary mystique, a Zen-like discipline, but in the few examples of it that they were able to show me, the ad was always more arresting and more powerful than others in the same campaign.

Herb and Lou always strove to make ads on this model, and whenever they saw one made by someone else, it was cause for rejoicing. Most of these came from a young agency called Doyle Dane Bernbach that was doing bright, lively, incredibly smart work, mostly for little Jewish clients like El Al, Ohrbach's, Goodman's Matzohs, and Levy's Real Jewish Rye Bread.

I called Phyllis Robinson, Copy Chief at Doyle Dane Bernbach, and her secretary told me firmly not to even bother sending my portfolio.

One of the other places that consistently turned out smart work that Lou and Herb admired was Time, Inc. Its Sales Promotion Director, Nick Samstag, had earned a reputation as one of the great ad writers of the time, and it was said that his department was like a Harvard Graduate School for copywriters. A couple of years there and you could write your own ticket. I thought that my background in magazine promotion, slim though it was, might serve to get me in.

So I called Samstag and was told by his secretary that they weren't hiring but that I should send my resume for their files.

I sent the resume, but I really wanted to meet and talk to Nick Samstag, even if there were no job openings. I wanted to get his opinion of my work, his advice, maybe even some names of people I should call.

So I called again. And again and again.

His secretary, unfailingly polite, cheerful, and icy, always told me that Mr. Samstag was busy, in a conference, and out of town. What's more, he had just stepped out, wasn't taking calls from anyone today, was in an all-day meeting, and was making a major presentation.

After a couple of weeks, I got an idea. I arranged for the delivery of a caged carrier pigeon to Samstag's office. The note I wrote to go with it said, "I've been trying to get word in to you for weeks. It has just occurred to me that maybe you can't get word *out*. If you're in some kind of trouble and need help, put a message in the capsule on the pigeon's leg and toss the bird out of the window."

The pigeon came back. The note read, "Call me. I'll talk to you. N.S."

It wasn't much of a message, but those capsules are pretty small.

I never did get to work for Nick Samstag, but I did get to see him. I learned a valuable lesson from him, too. On his wall hung a framed sign that read: L.I.N.E. He explained that it stood for Logic Is Not Enough. "The logic had better be there," he said, "but if you don't go beyond it, you'll make some damn bad advertising."

He must have written some good comments on my interview card, because it wasn't long after our meeting that I was hired by Gene Wolfe, who was Promotion Director for *House & Home*, one of Time, Inc.'s more obscure magazines. *House & Home* was a spinoff from *Architectural Forum*. It was not a consumer magazine, but was edited for professional homebuilders, residential architects, land developers, mortgage lenders, and suppliers to the homebuilding industry.

Gene assumed that my background at the *American Home* magazine—which was all about decorating, cooking, gardening, and crafts—was perfect grounding for *House & Home*. I didn't correct him, acted like a person who knew all about the building trades, and got the job.

Time, Inc. was a friendly place. People came around to welcome me and introduce themselves. Everyone always seemed to have time to chat. Among the first to come around was a man who looked like Ignatz Mouse in the old "Krazy Kat" comic strip. His name was Bob Murray, and he was an editor who specialized in sewage. "It's ten-thirty," he said. "Coffee break time. You want to go out and start to get to know each other?"

We went down to the 48th Street exit and walked across the

street to a bar called GGG, pronounced Three Gees. "I always have a martini at coffee breaks," Bob explained. "Care to join me? My treat."

I said sure, and I asked what he drank when it was time to have a martini.

"Three martinis," he said.

I learned after a few weeks of a growing friendship with Bob, Walt Wagner, and other staffers not to go out until the afternoon coffee break, which came at about three-thirty. I had learned that I couldn't work very well after a *House & Home* coffee break, but by three in the afternoon it was okay, because there was never any work left to do anyhow.

In fact there was very little work at any time. Time, Inc. believed in overstaffing in order to avoid understaffing or overworking during the summer when everyone took at least a month's vacation. Time, Inc. also believed in sociability. Solitary lunches were unheard of, short lunches were rare, and lunching at one's desk all but forbidden.

It was a lovely place to work.

That spring I went on my first business trip. I was taken along with the space salesmen to Bermuda to attend a three-day sales meeting, plus a free weekend following it. We stayed at the Mid Ocean Club, an elegant and exclusive private hotel whose beautiful little pink sand beach with a great natural arch of coral was always shown in Bermuda tourist advertising. There was no way an ordinary tourist would ever get to see it.

Our group was as ordinary as tourists could be at the Mid Ocean, but we were billed as guests of famed publisher Henry Luce, so it was okay. Our rooms all had small brass plaques on their doors, each with the name of some famous person who had slept there. My room, named for a British peer, was between Winston Churchill's and Franklin Roosevelt's from the time they met in Bermuda for what was not as yet called a summit.

My lordly room was large and airy, with a fine view of the golf course and the sea. On the bedside table was a tray with an ice bucket, some glasses, and a bottle of Bushmills Irish Whiskey. With it was a note that read, "Here's to a good meeting and the time to have some fun, too." It was signed, "Harry."

Harry? I didn't know anyone named Harry. I didn't know anyone at all, except Ellen, who knew that I liked Irish whiskey and that Bushmills was my favorite brand. I don't think I had ever ordered it at a bar and only drank it at home. I never offered it to guests, either, because it was too expensive.

I couldn't imagine who had sent me this bottle.

I went next door to Churchill's room to ask Bill Blanchard, one of the space salesmen, if he could help me with the puzzle. Next to his bed was the same sort of ice bucket and glasses, a bottle of Beefeater Gin, and the same note.

Bill told me that Harry was what Mr. Luce was called by his friends, never Henry.

"But he's not my friend," I said. "I've never met him, and even if *you* have, I'll bet you don't call him Harry. And how does he know what I like to drink? I've only been working here six weeks."

"Time, Inc. is in the business of information gathering," Bill said.

I went to my room and sipped some Bushmills, straight, no ice, and looked out at the sea. Despite the balmy breeze, I felt chilled. If Henry Luce's intelligence department had gone to the trouble of learning what I liked to drink, what else had they learned? That I'd been a left wing student activist? That I'd been a member of the Political Action Committee of the National Maritime Union? These would be black marks in our rather conservative company. As I thought about it, I was less concerned about how deeply they had probed than I was about how deeply and how long they would continue to probe in the years ahead.

I knew then that I had to leave this job as soon as I decently could. Maybe a year, maybe two. I had been job-hopping too fast and needed to stay in one place for a while. Okay, two years. It wouldn't be hard.

But it would never again seem a lovely place to work.

It did have its pleasant moments, apart from our tipsy coffee breaks and occasional weekends with Bob and Betty Murray at their lakeside home in Rockland County. There were other people, too, and always parties. Adrian Taylor was the magazine's Art Director, and his parties were always made special by the presence of his neighbor, a chubby and manic young aspiring comedian named Jonathan Winters who came on early and strong and kept coming on till the last of us tottered out.

"Visualize it," I remember him saying with begging intensity, "this man just *loved* canaries, loved them passionately, sexually." His hands fluttered wildly in front of his pants. "The only trouble was getting them to hold still."

There were interesting moments associated with the work, too.

I wrote a speech for Perry Prentice, *House & Home*'s publisher. Time, Inc. owner Henry Luce liked it and asked me to write a speech about land use and cluster housing for him. He liked it, too, and I began to write speeches for him from time to time. This meant that I was occasionally included in his entourage.

I had lunch one day with Henry Luce and Frank Lloyd Wright.

I used to put it that way when I was trying to impress people, sort of sliding over the fact that there were five other people at the table and that I, as the junior member, didn't even attempt to get into the conversation.

Luce had been a fan of Wright's for years and used to say, not at all jokingly, that he only published *Architectural Forum* to give Wright a showcase and keep his slightly fading reputation alive.

During the lunch, Luce said to Wright that Time's quarters at 9 Rockefeller Plaza had become a little cramped and outmoded for us and that he had been considering building a place of our own, something contemporary, lots of glass, maybe even put in central air conditioning. He asked if Wright would consider designing it for him.

Wright said that he would do it without a fee, providing Luce would meet one small condition, and that if Luce wouldn't meet it, he wouldn't design it for any price.

"What condition, Frank?" Luce asked warily.

"Don't build it in this city. Build it in Westchester or Connecticut, even in New Jersey, but I don't want ever again to design a building to be erected in this city."

Construction was then under way on the Guggenheim Museum, which Luce liked to call "Frank's Bendix." (To understand this, you have to be old enough to know what washing machines used to look like.)

"New York building codes force the museum design, Frank?" Luce asked.

Wright said that he had found plenty of ways around them and that he was perfectly satisfied with his museum, but that it sure would have looked better in a meadow. "How about it?" he asked. "Don't you want a Frank Lloyd Wright masterpiece of your own? For no architectural fee? Just buy the right meadow, and it's yours."

Luce stammered (he always stammered) that it just wouldn't be a practical thing to do, that we were, after all, dependent on our sales forces, and that they had to be within easy reach of advertisers and their agencies, and where would we get the clerical staff from if we were out in the country? And, besides. . . .

Wright cut in. "Harry," he said, "I never thought I'd see the day when you were frightened of doing something original." Then, most unexpectedly, he turned to me. He was looking, I guess, for a young person to address as a student.

"There is nothing so timid," he said deliberately, "as a million dollars."

That was when a million dollars was something.

I tried again to get into Doyle Dane Bernbach. This time, I at least got a chance to bring my book in for a review by Phyllis Robinson, a famous Copy Chief by now. (Creative directors still hadn't been invented.)

Phyllis went through the book carefully and sadly. "I'm afraid there's no place for you here," she said, closing the book gently as one would lower the lid of a coffin.

Something in her manner made me ask, "Now or never?"

She smiled kindly. "I think I mean never."

The one great perk at *House & Home* was plenty of free time. I used it to support my growing family by free lancing on anything I could get.

Bill Alley was a producer of industrial films who gave me a chance to write some scripts for him. The first, I remember, was a half hour film for Blue Coal, then a well-known brand of home-heating coal. Blue Coal is a subject that's hard to talk about for five minutes, because all it was was commodity coal that had been sprayed with a blue-tinted coating. Somehow I managed to write up a half hour's commentary, and Bill Alley thought it was a pretty good script, after I'd done a couple of rewrites. He told me to send him a bill.

I asked him how much I should charge.

"Whatever you think's right," he said. "If I think it's too much, I'll let you know."

The thing had taken me about twenty hours to write. I was earning $8,000 a year at Time, Inc., which worked out at a little under $4.50 an hour, figuring a 35-hour week. So if I charged at my salary rate, the script should go for $90, or actually a little less. But I figured what the hell, let's go the distance. I sent a bill for $100.

He paid it promptly and gave me another assignment, this one a script for Westinghouse substations.

It took a lot of reading just to understand what a substation was. To do my homework involved learning almost a whole new language. The actual writing was the hardest piece of work I had ever done or ever would do. It took me a little over forty hours, so it should have been worth $200, but to compensate for the pain I asked for $300. The check came in the return mail.

A couple of months later I got another assignment, and although it was a pretty easy job, I set the price higher. There was no complaint.

By the time I had been writing for Bill Alley for more than a year, I began to get the feeling that I didn't quite understand how free-lance writing was priced. I found out who in Nick Samstag's department was responsible for film production and asked what the price ought to be for an average half-hour industrial film script.

The range, it turned out, was between $1,000 and $1,500. The last one I had done had earned me $800. No wonder Bill always paid me promptly and put up with each price increase.

When I completed my next script for him, I sent an invoice for $1,200.

"You finally got it right" said the note that accompanied the check.

I can't remember how this next event started, but I somehow found myself one of a group of free lancers, moonlighters really, who were working for a dynamic and charming paranoiac named Gerry Schaflander, who had conceived the tobaccoless cigarette.

This was in 1956, some seven years before the U.S. Surgeon General first issued a warning linking cigarettes to cancer, but everybody already knew that this was the case, in some way as yet to be determined.

We pointed out to Gerry that tobacco may have nothing to do with the problem. Maybe it was the paper or the glue. Maybe it didn't matter what you burned, we argued. Maybe just inhaling enough of any smoke will cause cancer. A scientifically literate member of the group thought that the carcinogen (a new word for us) might be the hydrocarbons, in which case it would be as we said. We all felt very smart and went around muttering about hydrocarbons and carcinogens.

"That's all beside the point," Gerry said. "We're never going to mention the word cancer. Do you think we want our asses sued off? All we're going to sell is a cigarette with no tobacco. And with no health claims. The public will draw its own conclusions, which may even be true."

We free lancers were actually partners in the venture because Gerry had no money to pay us with. We each had shares of stock, and if Gerry's worst-case scenario for the minimum share of market came to pass, we would all become pretty rich. So we put in a lot of effort. We met almost every day during lunch time in Gerry's sketchily furnished offices to wrestle with our first problem—naming the cigarette. Without that we couldn't get started on package design, advertising, sales promotion, publicity, and other chores that attend the launching of a product.

Gerry was strong for names like Notobac, Nicotex, and the like, all of which sounded to us like patent medicines. We wanted a name that sounded like a cigarette, something a smoker wouldn't be embarrassed to order or to be seen smoking. We finally won our point. The cigarette was named Vanguard.

The name *Vanguard* had a leading-edge quality and a good-looking *V* to anchor the logo that looked great on the package and carton we designed. The name seemed to give our advertising and promotion roughs the look of authenticity and authority.

We were ready to go, as soon as we had a product.

The chemists were having a tough time finding a substance that would burn like tobacco. Some things flared up in a sudden dry blaze. Others smoldered weakly in a dim, damp fire like peat. I remember one vegetable mixture (we were using salads by then) that burned more or less at the rate of tobacco, but its coal produced a heat so intense that it was uncomfortable to hold the cigarette after it had burned down more than half an inch.

One of the problems that the chemists faced was that the weed couldn't be a weed. It had to be a currently farmed cash crop in order to assure them of a source of supply.

Eventually they came up with the answer. It was a secret blend of leafy crops, but the principal ingredient, nearly 90 percent of the blend, was alfalfa.

Alfalfa was cheap and plentiful. When properly cured, it burned very much like tobacco. There was nothing wrong with it except the taste, which was disgusting, and the aroma, which was worse.

The chemists assured us that taste and aroma were not going to be a problem once the specialized flavor and fragrance chemists got hold of the product. Those people were magicians, they said. They could make anything taste and smell like anything else, they said. Not only could they give alfalfa the taste and aroma of tobacco, but they could duplicate any popular brand we wanted to knock off, given a little time for experiment and development.

But we didn't have a little time.

Gerry Schaflander was convinced that others, especially the big tobacco companies, were already working on similar projects. We had to get out there first, and fast, or they'd eat our lunch.

I pointed out that the tobacco companies had a big investment in tobacco, and that's what they were interested in selling. If he really wanted to worry, he should worry about the big alfalfa companies, but he didn't buy it.

"Those guys are in the cigarette business, not the tobacco business," he said. "If it looks like tobacco's going to be a problem, they'll make cigarettes with anything that burns and sells, just like us. If we're not out there first to build some brand loyalty, we're dead." He puffed nervously at his Vanguard.

I commented that he was the only smoker on earth who was able to stand Vanguards and that the surest way to kill the idea was to market them in their present state of development.

"Have you tried this batch? Number V-27B?" He held out the package. "Go on, try one. They're great!"

I lit up cautiously and even inhaled a little. It was indeed slightly less horrid than its predecessors, but there was a new quality that I discovered after smoking it about halfway down. It made me lightheaded and giddy, but not in a pleasant way because the giddiness included more than a hint of nausea.

Gerry took a deep, satisfied puff and smiled benignly. "That's our product," he said. "That's the one we're taking to market."

I didn't learn until after the whole tobaccoless cigarette story was history that Gerry had never in his life smoked anything until Vanguard.

We rushed into test market with V-27B. Smokers rushed into stores to buy Vanguards by the carton, and the next day rushed back to return nine and three-quarter packs.

The advertising and promotion moonlighters had a small defeat party at Ratazzi's, sharing a general glow of low spirits, when a ray of hope appeared. Paul Kirshon, who was head of the Sales Promotion Department at Doyle Dane Bernbach, was one of the group of moonlighters. He came over to say that he had really enjoyed working with me and asked if I would like to come to work for him at DDB.

"Do you have to go through Phyllis Robinson?" I asked.

Paul told me, somewhat huffily, that he ran his own department and was allowed to do his own hiring. All that was required was that I be approved by Bill Bernbach, which would be more or less pro forma.

I was ecstatic. Doyle Dane Bernbach at last! So what if it was only in Sales Promotion? I would be brilliant. I would do such great work that in no time I would be invited to write national copy. I didn't care that I was entering through the back door; it was a door, and it was open.

The next day I reviewed my portfolio with Paul. He helped me edit and reorganize it, throwing out some things, moving others to more prominent positions, relegating others to the back of the book. When he was satisfied, he called Bernbach and set up an appointment that afternoon.

I met Bill Bernbach, not in his office, but in a little conference room used by the Creative Department. After I had waited nervously in that bleak little room for about half an hour, he came in, greeted me grumpily, and pulled the portfolio toward him.

He was a small man whose hair, complexion, and clothing all appeared to be a nearly colorless shade of grey. Out of this background, his blue eyes were singularly noticeable and commanding.

He was in shirtsleeves, and his hands were dirty with what may have been proving ink. To people who knew Bill Bernbach, this must sound almost as bizarre as if I had said that he was wearing Bermuda shorts.

He flipped a page in my book, leaving black smudges on a proof.

He flipped through some more pages pretty quickly, leaving more smudges.

I was getting angry, but I only said, as mildly as possible, that he may have had the wrong idea of what position I was being reviewed for, that I was a copywriter, not an art director.

"I mean," I said, "that you can't just look at these ads, you've got to slow down a little and read them."

He looked up from the book and stared at me, his pale blue eyes as hard as ice. "I'm reading all I need to," he said frostily.

I slammed the book shut with his hand still in it.

"You can go fuck yourself," I said.

I called Paul Kirshon from the pay phone in the downstairs lobby to tell him that I guessed I would never be able to work for Doyle Dane Bernbach.

Herb Lubalin's studio operation at Sudler & Hennessey was doing more than designing ads to sell drugs to doctors. It was also establishing Herb as one of the outstanding graphic designers in the country. The look of his pharmaceutical advertising and of his experimental work using type as a design element was already a major influence on art directors at DDB and other smart young agencies.

My free-lance work with Herb was never on pharmaceuticals but on ads for the studio, which he ran as a separate profit center. These ads were little lessons in design, usually on the innovative use of typography.

I was working with him on one of these ads one night, and when we had finished (the headline was "Ugh!ly?"), Herb told me that the agency had decided to set up a consumer division.

He said that he had already hired an exciting young designer named George Lois to be Head Art Director of the division and asked me if I would like to be Copy Chief.

"There's room for more than one Doyle Dane," Herb said. "In fact, there is room for exactly two."

I went home on air, told Ellen about it, and the next day went smiling to Time, Inc. to resign. I had been there for two years, a continuity record I was not to break very often in my career.

Resigning from Time, Inc. was a curious ceremony.

The company didn't like to have people resign; they took it as a sign of their own failure, and the only thing they hated more was having to fire anyone. Gene Wolfe, my boss, took it pretty well, but insisted that I talk to Personnel before actually making a commitment. I told him that I was already committed, but he said that I owed it to the company to give Personnel a fair hearing before I cut myself off.

I saw the Personnel Director, a man with the endearing name of Dudley Darling. He had my dossier on his desk. In any other company I would have called it a file, but I'm sure that at Time, Inc. it was a dossier.

"You've had three excellent semiannual reviews," he told me, "and we do hate to lose good people. Do you mind if I try to talk you out of leaving us?"

He took a worksheet from the dossier and unfolded it. It was a wide, pale green piece of graph paper covered with small, handwritten numbers, and it must have taken hours to write. (Computers *had* been invented, but they were the size of locomotives and were not for office use.)

"This sheet represents a projection of your career earnings in order to determine the amount of your pension," Darling explained. "I won't take you through the whole thing unless you want me to, but for now, let's just look at the bottom line."

He turned the sheet around for me to read and pointed at a figure. It was $42,000.

"That would be the amount of your annual pension if you work with us until the age of sixty. The minimum amount," he corrected himself.

He expanded on what the worksheet showed. I was then twenty-nine years old, and Personnel had projected my earnings for each year between then and sixty, based on merely acceptable performance, coupled with merely acceptable corporate profits, and minimal annual raises.

The spectre of Sears Roebuck rose before me.

Personnel hadn't worked out what I would earn and what my pension would be if I were actually to be a success, because they knew, and Darling shared with me, the fact that success was unpredictable. Even at Time, Inc.

It was pretty impressive, considering my then salary of $9,000.

But, of course, that was what was wrong with it. I explained to Dudley Darling that the fact that the worksheet was there, that they had actually manufactured such a thing, was terribly depressing to me.

"You've got my whole life worked out," I told him, "and I can't imagine anything more boring. That's exactly why I want to leave; I'm bored, and I want my life to be exciting."

"The only truly exciting thing is danger," Darling said. "If you want your wife and children to be safe, you must prepare to be bored."

MORE STEPPING STONES

George Lois was a tall Greek kid with a big nose and a big, lopsided grin. He looked as if he'd been nailed together from scrap building materials. The loose-limbed way he walked and the way he talked with his hands, his shoulders hunched over, gave me the impression that he'd be generally sloppy.

He wasn't sloppy. He was compulsively neat. No one knows better than I how neat he was because I shared a small office with him.

George's drawing board, work table, and taboret were each a precise layout. Every tool of the art director's craft was in exactly the same place each day, and each item was exactly parallel to or at right angles with the next. Everything in our office, including my desk and typing table, was aligned in a perfect Swiss-school-of-design grid.

I didn't mind it. I've always been pretty neat myself. But I did like to keep my telephone at an angle on the right side of my desk so that the dial faced me. George didn't like that angle. He never spoke to me about it because he must have known how dumb it would have sounded, but whenever he passed my desk, he would surreptitiously straighten the phone to make it sit parallel with the edge of the desk.

George's layouts were as neat and squared as Mondrian paintings. He liked to set copy so that each line had exactly the same character count with no incomplete lines, called widows. In order to do this, we would set the copy in the usual way, and then I would cut, add, or rewrite as necessary, keeping a careful character count of each line. Then we'd get a second typesetting and see how close we had come. Usually we had to go on to a third or even a fourth setting before we had it so that the look pleased George and the flow and sense of the copy still pleased me.

Looking back on that time, I can no longer find any justification for working like that, but it seemed to make sense then. It was so time-consuming and so expensive that it would have maddened most clients, but lucky for us, we didn't have any clients.

Most of our work was done on speculation in an attempt to get some piece of business. We had hired on a half-time basis a half-writer, half-account man named Fred Papert who had a talent for opening doors. He kept us busy pitching, often working with us as a writer/idea man. Fred had many talents and an easy charm as a presenter, but I think we must have been nearly impossible to sell.

For one thing, George had a way of making clients nervous. If they appeared to have any doubts about our work, he could be counted on to say something like "You fuckin' crazy? This is the best fuckin' campaign you ever saw in your fuckin' life." This speech was usually delivered in a tone of mixed fury and contempt while George loomed over the client with fists clenched.

The kind of advertising we were making also had a way of making clients nervous. I remember one campaign we presented to Arpège perfume. They had asked us to come up with a series of ads to run in *Seventeen* magazine, whose readers are mostly about thirteen years old. The client's idea was to get these kids to think that Arpège was the greatest stuff in the world while they were still a few years away from using perfume.

Our first ad for this tender audience was a photo of a birthday cake with sixteen candles blazing in the dark. The line read, "Are you woman enough for Arpège?"

The client thought that this just might be a little suggestive for so young an audience.

"It certainly is," George agreed. "It suggests that if they could get their hands on some Arpège they could get laid."

"But these girls are only thirteen!" the client wailed.

"I don't get your point," George said.

We finally got a real, live client, maybe not ideal for what we did, but we were excited by the prospect of actually having ads run somewhere. The account was a discount department store called Carr's, and it was located somewhere in New Jersey, in one of the Oranges. I drove out there a lot and should remember which one, but I never found the same route twice and was always amazed to arrive at the store. New Jersey has always been my Bermuda Triangle.

Our ads for Carr's had great presence and didn't look at all like ads for a discount store. They had big, arresting photos, bright, provocative, and sometimes witty headlines, and the product descriptions, sometimes as many as twenty in one ad, all were set in exactly the same number of lines, each with equal numbers of characters and with no widows.

Since Carr's needed four ads a week, the work load was staggering. We worked twelve to fourteen hours a day, me writing, cutting, and rewriting while George sliced words apart with a razor blade to take out spaces between letters.

We needed help. George took a kid named Sam Scali out of the bullpen and made him an art director. (I'm not going to tell you, not even later on, how Sam made it from there to becoming very rich with Scali, McCabe and Sloves. He can write his own book.)

Then we got the Land Rover and Rover automobile account. Herb Lubalin designed the ads, most of which showed a Land Rover climbing over a rugged and dangerous-looking mountain of type. I wrote the copy to fit the layout exactly, of course, with no widows and no word breaks. I began to develop a strong dislike for the Swiss.

Then we got business from Amstel Beer, and we hired Bob Fiore, another talented young art director. And I was still the only copywriter, writing and rewriting and rewriting every ad for all four of them. I learned how to work pretty fast.

It was all very heady, and we all had great spirit, enthusiasm, and unlimited optimism. Until the accounts began to disappear as fast as they had appeared.

Land Rover and Rover couldn't get enough dealers, so they pulled out of the U.S. market.

Carr's decided that what they really needed was tough,

schlocky, screamer ads like all the other discount stores had. They thought rightly that we didn't know how to do that kind of work.

The Arpège project never became a reality.

Amstel Beer concluded that there was no room for two Heinekens in the United States.

And we began to wonder if there was really room for two Doyle Dane Bernbachs.

Arthur Sudler asked George and me if we'd work on some ethical pharmaceutical business to help pay our salaries.

We liked the idea of selling drugs to doctors, though we hated most of the advertising the agency was turning out. It was all beautifully designed, of course, with great illustrations and photography and some stunning use of type. But the writing was technical, scientific, stuffy, flat, and self-consciously dignified.

We knew this was wrong, or at least hopelessly outdated. We both had friends our own ages who were doctors, and none of them were technical, scientific, stuffy, and dignified. In fact, their idea of humor was generally pretty raunchy.

We thought that doctors would make a great audience for advertising. They were human beings, not gods, but they were highly educated and very smart. They were also, like most human beings, funny, sexy, emotional, and illogical. If we only appealed to them through their human qualities, we would make advertising that would be different from anything else they had ever seen. It would be noticed, remembered, and effective. We talked Art Sudler into letting us take this radical new humanistic approach.

Unfortunately, the first product we were asked to work on was a treatment for hemorrhoids.

We did an ad that has become one of the best-known ads that never ran, a familiar bad taste gag: "Kiss bloody piles good-bye!"

The only thing that kept us from getting fired was that Art Sudler was pretty sure we were only kidding. But he was just unsure enough to take us off the business and assign it to a conventional drug creative team.

Our new account was Lanteen Vaginal Gel and Diaphragms.

Lanteen was a well-established product. The doctors knew of it and thought it was okay, so we were told we didn't have to say much. Just show the tube of gel and the diaphragm in its kit, make the logo big enough, and come up with "a clever, catchy line."

The first ad we submitted read, "Fecund to none."

That never made it to the client.

The account executive gave us some new direction. "Look, even though the docs are aware of Lanteen, they may not know everything about it. So let's do an ad that includes most of the selling features, okay?"

The selling points were ease of insertion, super-smooth gel, a nice fragrance, a good-looking kit, and a few things I can't remember any more. We agreed to do an ad that got them all in.

The result was a black page with a long, narrow, white outline speech balloon inside which was white type. The copy, written in a sort of breathless feminine style, was an outpouring of praise for Lanteen gel and diaphragms.

Alongside the bottom of this was a small speech balloon with copy that read, "Shut up and kiss me."

We made the account guy agree to let us present it to the client because it was absolutely on strategy, sold hard, and had what we thought was a nice little twinkle in its eye.

The client thought it was dirty. He also thought we didn't have to do all that selling, and he gave us some specific direction. "Just get the name Lanteen out there. No copy, no headline. Only the name, in a way they'll remember."

We could see that he was trying to tie our hands, so, just using the name of the product, we made a really dirty ad.

It was two speech balloons in the dark again. They were both the same size. One said, "Lanteen Jelly?" and the other said, "Lanteen Jelly."

Art Sudler looked for something else for us to work on.

This probably sounds like college humor, horsing around, a couple of irresponsible juniors at play, but it really wasn't. We were trying hard to do something new, looking for new ways to marry words and graphics in an attempt to engage the reader's attention and hook a message into his memory.

Only the pun, "fecund to none," could be brushed aside as kid stuff, and we sure didn't fight for its life. We knew it wasn't what we were aiming for. But the other ads using the speech balloons in the dark used graphics in a new way. We knew we were on to something, and we saw that some of the people at Doyle Dane Bernbach were on to the same thing, but none of us had quite gotten the hang of it yet. So far all we had done was make our account execs and clients nervous and suspicious.

We had seen one perfect example of our kind of advertising, and it had come from Doyle Dane Bernbach. It was an ad for El Al airlines that was a full-page photo of the ocean with a strip a couple of inches wide torn off the right side. The headline said that the Atlantic Ocean was now 20 percent smaller. What a way to announce a slightly faster flight!

Bill Taubin was the Art Director, and Bill Bernbach the Copywriter. Years later, when Taubin was asked how that famous ad came about, he said, "I was tearing oceans in my office when Bernbach came in."

George and I wanted to do work like that: pure, totally unexpected, crystal-clear with complete interdependence of visual and verbal elements.

We were feeling our way, but we were still much too involved with typography, under the influence and inspiration of Herb Lubalin. One campaign we did was for a medicine called Dimetane. We set an ad with a large headline that read "SWELLING" and then mounted the ad on a cylinder and photographed it so the page in the magazine looked as if it were bulging up at the reader. Another in the series was "ITCHING," and George had simply scratched the type so the white showed through. I guess these things sound pretty tame and predictable today, but then, nobody had ever seen anything like that campaign.

We were so typographically turned on that George and I created a Christmas card for the use of both of our families that was a pure typographic joke. It was a long message that incorporated a lot of words that had *HO*s in them. The words were in green except for the *HO*s, which were in red, so the card sort of chuckled at you like Santa Claus.

To give you something of the effect, I'll boldface the *HO*s.

WISHING YOU A **HO**LIDAY OF **HO**SPITALITY & **HO**T TODDIES & CHOCOLATES & **HO**NEY CAKES: CHOIRS OF CHORISTERS (**HO**LY POLYPHONY!) SHOPS FULL OF **HO**BBYHORSES, **HO**OPS & SNOW-SHOVELS: A **HO**USE FULL OF **HO**LLYWREATHS, HAWT**HO**RNES & RHODODENDRONS: **HO**SANNAHS OF **HO**PE & T**HO**USANDS OF W**HO**LESOME THOUGHTS.

Not only did I find all those hidden *HO*s, which was hard enough, but the type was set flush left and right in a nice, perfectly square block without a widow and with only one word break, a hyphenated *rhodo-dendron.*

It was worth doing right because it was that perfect marriage of words and graphics that embodied an idea we held with religious fervor.

There was nothing wrong with the idea. We were sure there was nothing wrong with us, either, but a year slipped by and, with the exception of eight or ten ads for Carr's, we had done no consumer advertising.

George was the first to decide that it was hopeless. With no trouble at all he got a job at Doyle Dane Bernbach. I stayed behind, of course, and sulked.

Fred Papert was the next to give up on Sudler & Hennessey. He opened an ad agency with an art director named Bill Free.

Papert & Free started in style with smart offices in the brand-new Seagram building. They had a couple of clients, just about enough to pay the rent, and they had a staff loaded with talent and the explosive potential of a hip flask full of nitroglycerine. The staff consisted of their wives, Diane Papert and Marcella Free.

In short order, Sam Scali followed George to DDB. Bob Fiore went somewhere else, starting on a path that would lead him to become one of the top creative directors in the business. And I stayed on, doing little house ads about typographic design with Herb.

Then one day, through some contact of Herb's, we were named the agency for Victor Borge's Rock Cornish Game Hens, a mail-order business the comedian was trying to build on his vast farm in Connecticut.

"This is what we've been waiting for," Herb said. "This can be a real showcase. He wants to advertise in *The New Yorker*."

Borge wanted to see us the next day at nine in the morning. His farm in Southbury, Connecticut, was a two-and-a-half-hour drive. We agreed to go in the company car, actually Art Sudler's Jaguar, leaving from the office at six in the morning. That meant I had to leave home at about five o'clock.

We arrived a little early, to be told by the housekeeper, speaking through a screen door, that Mr. Borge was out for his morning ride and should be back soon. We were not invited into the house, but told to wait outside. We camped out on porch furniture, looked at the landscape, and listened for the sound of hooves.

When Borge hadn't showed up by ten o'clock, Herb rang the bell and asked the housekeeper if it was possible to get a cup of coffee as we hadn't had breakfast. She said no.

It was nearly eleven when Borge strolled over from the stables and accepted our introductions with no apology for keeping us waiting. He led us to the mail-order office in a shed just past the horse barn and introduced us to his business manager. This man, he told us, would take us on a brief tour of the chicken farm and then conduct a review of the advertising they had done so far, with a cost analysis of each ad. When that was finished, we were to come back to the house and see Borge.

All this was said in a curt, businesslike manner, without the least trace of humor.

The tour wasn't much. We looked at rock cornish game hens, which are just little chickens. We also looked at some pheasants and some quail, being bred as possible line extensions, plus a few peacocks that Borge had bought just for the hell of it.

Then we looked at ads and numbers: which ad pulled how many orders in what publications.

We learned that mail-order professionals evaluate results in terms of cost per order, not profit per order. They don't expect to make money on an ad, but they look for as low a cost as possible. They're willing to pay something for an order because they figure that they've bought themselves a customer, someone who shops by mail and, better yet, someone who shops by mail from them. They figure to make up the cost and make a profit by repeat orders, response to special direct mailings, and catalogs full of related items. For instance, since we were selling to people who thought of themselves as gourmet cooks, we might follow up with offers of game jellies, herbs and spices, cookware, and kitchen gadgets.

The tour of the poultry, the analysis of the ads, and the lecture on mail-order economics took about an hour and a half. Although we were starving, we thought we'd best go back to the house and turn ourselves in to Mr. Borge.

"Oh, no," we were told by the housekeeper. "Mr. Borge and the family are just about ready to sit down for lunch. You can wait here on the porch."

Herb asked her if there was some village nearby where we could get something to eat. She said no.

Borge finally joined us at about two-thirty. He spent less than fifteen minutes telling us how to make advertising and said that he expected to see ideas, layouts, and copy in one week. He left without shaking hands. He didn't make even one little joke.

We worked hard and fast and created some classy-looking ads that didn't look at all like regular mail-order advertisements. Designed to run in such magazines as *The New Yorker* and *Gourmet*, they were editorial-looking ads a full column deep.

The copy was written in an upscale, conversational manner with a few little jokes scattered among the selling points. They were signed with Victor Borge's autograph.

On the day we were ordered to be there, Borge again told us to show up at nine in the morning and again kept us waiting till two. But he bought the campaign. He even liked the jokes. He even smiled at one.

A couple of months later, Borge asked us to come back to talk about the introduction of pheasants and quail to the line and the creation of a Victor Borge Game Bird Cook Book—at nine AM again.

Once more the housekeeper told us that Mr. Borge was out for his morning ride and would be back shortly. This time we were prepared. We sat at a picnic table under a tree and breakfasted on fruit, bagels, and lox and cream cheese we had brought in a basket. We lingered over Danish and coffee. By eleven, Borge had still not showed up.

Just for the sake of making conversation, certainly with no serious intent, I said, "I'm sick of this waiting around. Let's get them to saddle up horses, and we'll ride after him."

"I can't ride a horse," Herb said. "Can you?"

"Sure I can."

Our account exec, Bernie Turock, hurriedly put in his disclaimer of riding ability, so I said I was prepared to go it alone.

Herb asked me to stop a moment and visualize what I was proposing. "Think how ridiculous you'd look," he said. "A guy in a business suit hanging on to the horse with one hand and a presentation case with the other, galloping down the trail to try to head a comedian off at the pass."

Put that way, it suddenly became irresistible. I wanted to do it, if only to be able to tell the story in years to come. I got up and headed for the stables.

I ordered a stable boy to saddle me up a fast horse, and pronto. He said he'd do no such thing. Meanwhile, Herb and Bernie were tugging at me and telling me to stop being an idiot.

The stable master came running over to see what all the fuss was about. I again demanded a horse and emphasized the importance of running down Mr. Borge before we missed important magazine closing dates. The stable master recognized right away that he was dealing with a nut. He grabbed a pitchfork, stood with his back against the stable door, and pointed the fork at my navel.

"Don't make one move," he said.

"He was only joking," Herb explained. I thought it was time to agree with him. "That's right, just a little Madison Avenue humor," I laughed. "We'll just go back to the porch and wait for Mr. B., like we always do."

"Don't take one step," growled the stable master. "Not forward or backwards or any way You just stand right where you are till the boss comes back."

And that was the tableau Borge found a half hour later when he rode into the stable yard.

We decided to laugh it off rather than try to explain it. "It was just a joke,' Herb said, "but that guy has no sense of humor."

Borge looked at him very seriously and said, "You shouldn't ever joke with the help. They usually don't understand, and if they do, it makes them get too familiar."

So that was it. I now understood his attitude toward us. We were the help.

After our meeting with Borge, I went to see the business manager in his shed. Ellen had asked me if I could pick up some game hens at cost. He said he'd be glad to do that for me, sent someone to get a box of a dozen, and got out a worksheet to figure out the price

"On a cost-per-order basis," he smiled, "that will come to $328.80, which is $27.40 per bird."

I guess the public just wasn't ready either for little chickens by mail or for high-class mail-order advertising.

Herb told me that Lou Dorfsman was looking for a writer to work with him at CBS Radio and that both of them had decided that I should take the job because Sudler & Hennessey's Consumer Division was a dead game hen anyway.

Dorfsman was already recognized as one of the leading art directors and graphic designers in the United States, and I jumped at the chance to work with him full time. Even if it wasn't an ad agency, I knew that working with Lou would add enough good samples to my book, together with what I had done with George and Herb, to get me a real job next. At almost any agency except Doyle Dane Bernbach.

Our job at CBS had two parts. There was the job of advertising to the public to get them to tune in to a particular show and there was the even harder job of advertising to media buyers and clients to get them to buy time on CBS Radio. Finding reasons for either wasn't easy.

By 1959 television was the big news. Network radio was dying.

In 1950 when I first began trying to get into advertising, TV was scarcely a factor, and it never occurred to me that copywriting could or would ever include writing TV commercials. Only 10 percent of all homes in the United States owned a TV set, which made it less of an advertising medium than outdoor billboards. But in only nine years, TV ownership had shot up to 86 percent, and advertisers wanted to put their money on "Gunsmoke" or "Wagon Train" or "Have Gun, Will Travel," which were the three top-rated shows.

Nobody, not the audience or advertisers, gave much of a damn about radio soap operas. Ours, which were "Our Gal Sunday," "The Romance of Helen Trent," and "As the World Turns," were grinding slowly to an end and would be taken off the air, all on one day, in only a few months.

Our biggest crowd pleaser was the Arthur Godfrey Show, and on his best day old Arthur couldn't collect a nationwide audience of one million. Oh, on TV he could do millions and millions, but not on old-fashioned steam radio.

It was hard to do ads to help support the Godfrey Show. Arthur still acted like a superstar, wouldn't keep photographer's appointments, wouldn't record a few words for a tune-in spot, and was generally impossible.

He was driven to work in a Rolls Royce that waited for hours for him outside the CBS Radio building on East 52nd Street. You couldn't miss it. Its license plate was GOD.

Dr. Frank Stanton, President of CBS, Inc., forced him to get another license plate by threatening to fire him under a clause in the contract that allowed him to do so if Godfrey acted in any way that was embarrassing to the network. He would have been glad to fire Godfrey because of the slipping ratings, and Arthur knew it, so the plate went instead.

He must have known, as everyone else did, that if there was a God of broadcasting, it wasn't him but a TV cowboy.

Despite the feeling of being on a slowly sinking ship, Lou and I did actually get some good work done, even in the unpromising arena of trade advertising. I remember doing an ad that was directed to the grocery trade, a success story for some brand of tuna that had made network radio its main medium. The ad showed a bankroll in an open tuna can with a headline that read, "Fancy chunk style money." It was a perfect example of what we believed in because neither the picture nor the headline meant a thing by itself. We were really beginning to get the hang of how to make the new advertising.

Just as we were getting it, Bill Golden, who was Lou Dorfsman's counterpart at CBS TV and who had designed the CBS Eye, died suddenly. Stanton asked Lou to take Golden's job in TV, a much more important spot.

He left me behind with the imposing title of Advertising Director, CBS Radio Network and Owned and Operated Stations.

So I acted like an Advertising Director.

Along with the title came a seat on the program committee, which I saw as my chance to revitalize network radio, to find a new reason for its existence, a new content and a new style. I started doing some heavy thinking about the problem.

The first program committee meeting that I attended was the one that killed off the last of the radio soap operas. Nobody had the least idea of what to do with the vacated time, so it reverted to the affiliate stations for local programming, mostly disk jockeys.

Radio was becoming a free jukebox. It was pretty easy to listen to because there were hardly any commercial interruptions.

For the next two months I spent almost all of my time working on a proposal for new programming that might save network radio. It was a mix of news, education, self-improvement, and inspirational programs, with nothing based on entertainment because there was no way radio could compete with TV as show business. TV was still so new that people considered the weather reports entertainment.

I could hardly wait for the next meeting of the program committee.

I brought my proposals in a set of neatly bound folders, one for each committee member. I had prepared charts and had an easel ready for my well-rehearsed presentation. I had everything worked out, right down to production costs, estimates of audience size and composition for each segment, advertiser prospect lists by category, the whole thing.

I waited through the routine business of the meeting, as befitted the committee's most junior member. When the agenda was gone through, Arthur Hull Hayes, President of the radio network, asked if there was any other new business, and I stood up.

"Mr. Hayes," I said, "I have some programming ideas that I would like to present to the committee."

Hayes stood up at the far end of the table and held out his hand toward me, palm flat forward like a traffic cop. "Stop!" he commanded. "I don't want to hear any ideas. Ideas cost money."

I went back to my office and called Lou Dorfsman to see if he could use me in TV. I figured that network radio was already dead—at least from the neck up.

THE INNER SANCTUM

"Funny you called," Lou said. "I was just thinking of you and didn't know if it was right to call you or not."

He went on to tell me that he had just gotten off the phone with Bill Bernbach, who had called to ask Lou if he knew a good copywriter who had an understanding of broadcast promotion. DDB had just picked up the ABC account and had no one on staff who knew how to do trade advertising for it. Lou had thought of me right away, but wasn't sure it was right to help steal me from CBS. But, since I was looking anyway. . . .

I thanked him, but said it was impossible for me to ever be hired by Bernbach. I told him what had happened in the last interview.

"So go see him anyway," Lou said. "Maybe he's forgotten your face. And if he remembers, what do you lose? You just give him a chance to tell *you* to go fuck yourself. Don't be a schmuck; give it a try. The guy you should call is named Leon Meadow."

I called Meadow and explained that Lou Dorfsman had sent me in response to a call from Mr. Bernbach. We made a date for early the next week. With no great hope, I started to review my portfolio.

I had very few ads that met the criterion of art/copy inseparability, and I had only a few others that I thought were really good work. In all, there were only about eight or nine pieces I thought measured up to the standards of Doyle Dane Bernbach. That sure wasn't a lot to show for more than seven years in and around the ad business since I'd left Gimbels. I decided I had to put in a lot more, just to show I could turn it out if I had to. But I had to find a smart way to show that I knew the difference between quality and quantity.

I spent the weekend building a new portfolio out of plywood. When it was done and painted, it looked like a big, thin radio. It had two knobs that were actually index tabs to the two sections of the box, a shallow section for the good ads and a deep one for the rest.

The knobs were labeled *Tone* and *Volume.*

Leon Meadow loved the portfolio, loved the eight or nine good ads, and said that as far as he was concerned I was hired. But first I had to see Phyllis Robinson.

Phyllis laughed happily at the portfolio gag, liked all the right things and said, "Where have you been all these years?" Then she said that as far as she was concerned, I was hired.

"Don't I have to see Mr. Bernbach?" I asked.

Phyllis explained that on any usual day, I would, but that this was the last day before Bernbach was to leave for a month's vacation in Italy. She didn't know if he could spare the time to see me but took my portfolio and went to show it to him.

She was back in ten minutes. "He hasn't time to see you, but he says he doesn't care what you look like, just hire you."

And that's when I started growing my moustache.

I was put in a windowless cubicle with a metal partition and no door, at the end of a dead-end corridor in an outlying suburb of the copy department. My neighbors were Bob Levenson, Monte Ghertler, Sue Brock, Bob Olsen, Rita Seldon, Adrienne Claiborne, and Margaret Fishback.

Margaret was the only one I'd ever heard of, and I was thrilled to meet her. She was a light verse poet whose work was published in the *Herald Tribune* and who had actually published a volume or two of verse.

Levenson was a quiet, pleasant young guy whose job it was to make dealer ads for Volkswagen by cutting David Reider's copy. (Julian Koenig, who had won fame for starting the VW campaign, was no longer at the agency. He had quit a short time before with George Lois to join Fred Papert when Papert & Free broke up. Papert Koenig Lois was starting to be noticed already.)

Levenson said that it was a lot harder to cut Reider's copy than Koenig's and that he was learning a lot because of it. "You could just take out a few sentences or a whole paragraph of Koenig's and it still worked just fine, but Reider's copy is like a brick wall." He showed me what he meant, and I suddenly knew a lot more about writing than I had known before.

That first day I was taken to lunch by Bob Olsen, who had an outside office with windows. I though he must be important, even though the windows just gave a view of an airshaft. Olsen was the lead writer on ABC, doing the tune-in ads. We went to a Chinese restaurant on 6th Avenue (The Avenue of the Americas still hadn't been invented), and, as we strolled, Bob asked me how I had gotten into DDB. I didn't tell him about the past rejections but just described my radio portfolio. He liked it a lot.

When we were seated, and when we had toasted to the future with the sort of terrible martini found only in Chinese restaurants, I asked Bob how long he had been there and how he had gotten in.

He, too, had been hired for the ABC account and had only been at DDB for two weeks. He had last been at Lennon & Newell, a notably uncreative agency, so I asked him what was in his portfolio that got him hired at our Holy of Holies.

"Well, I had been doing a lot of movie advertising, so I guess they figured I could do tune-in ads for TV shows," he said. "But what really interested Phyllis was the campaign that got me fired at L & N."

It seems that the agency had been assigned the account of Wolfschmidt Vodka and hadn't the faintest idea of what to do with it. They had very little experience in the spirits market and none at all with vodka, which in those days was still considered an exotic drink, to be taken with caution if at all.

They gave the account to Bob Olsen. He didn't have any liquor background, but he was a good writer and was also, to put it kindly, a heavy and eclectic drinker. He asked for a few bottles so he could figure out the best way to drink the stuff. They gave him a case.

He spent the next couple of weeks drinking his way through

the case in various combinations and finally showed up, announcing that he had a bad headache and a good campaign.

His theme was "If it isn't Wolfschmidt, it isn't breakfast."

It was all quite rational, he told them. "You mix that stuff with tomato juice or orange juice or grapefruit juice—breakfast stuff—and it goes down like you never noticed it."

He couldn't understand why they wouldn't buy it. He got stubborn and refused to do another campaign. They fired him. When he showed his portfolio to Phyllis Robinson, he had the Wolfschmidt ads up front. Bob said she hired him before going on to look at anything else.

When I got back to the agency, there were three job requisitions on my desk, a note asking me to call someone in Traffic for instructions, and a note telling me to go meet my art director, Sid Meyers.

ABC trade advertising was easy to do. We worked quickly, got fast approvals from the client, who I suspect just didn't give a damn about trade advertising and let us do whatever we wanted, and I found myself with too much time on my hands.

That wasn't the case with Sid, who was also working with Bob Olsen and who had to finish the ads for publications. I didn't know what to do and was afraid to hang around my office doing nothing. At the same time I couldn't hang around Sid, who was busy.

Olsen suggested that I call the Traffic Director, Ray Ponterotto, to tell him I was up for any work that needed doing.

Ray was delighted. The next day he brought me requisitions for an ad for Chemstrand nylon fiber, an ad for Buxton wallets, and a radio spot for Lane Furniture, which was mostly hope chests.

The next week Ray brought me a requisition for a whole new campaign for the *Book of Knowledge* and told me to go see the account man, John Blumenthal, for a briefing.

Blumenthal looked like he should be working for the *Book of Knowledge*. He was a slim, scholarly looking man with the manner of a good professor who wants to be likable but won't take any nonsense. He told me all about his kids' encyclopedia and what a pleasure it was to be selling a product he, and I, could be proud of.

I said that I was sure pleased too, but I wanted to do more than read the ads he had set out for me that showed the work for the past two or three years. I wanted a *Book of Knowledge* to mess around with and to let my seven-year-old daughter use to help her with her school work. Maybe I could get some fresh insights and make a smart new campaign.

Blumenthal thought that was a fine idea and immediately called the client to have them send a twelve-volume set to my home by messenger. He was excited about my having a smart seven-year-old who could read already, because the *Book* was advertised as being for children from seven to seventeen.

The *Book* arrived. Andy, my daughter, and I decided to look up what it could tell us about the moon, because they were starting to learn some basic astronomy in school. I looked in the index and found many, many entries for moon scattered throughout most of the volumes. We looked up a few, found some too advanced, some about moons other than ours, some irrelevant (like poems about the moon), and eventually one that seemed to tell Andy a few interesting things she could take to school.

As I tried during the next few days to use the book with her, Andy lost all interest in it. I grew to hate it. I finally told John Blumenthal that he'd have to find another copywriter because I didn't believe in the product, and I wouldn't work on it.

John was shocked, scandalized, horrified. The *Book of Knowledge* was the first and foremost children's encyclopedia, a greatly respected book, an institution. It was, moreover, a cornerstone account of the agency's and had always published advertising of the highest standards.

I was sure all this was true, I explained, but since I didn't think the thing was any damn good at all, there was no way I could write good ads for it.

John said that I would have to go with him to discuss this with Mr. Bernbach. Oh God, I thought, I've been working here only six weeks and haven't even met the man, and this will be some way to start with him. I wished my moustache had been given another month or two to fill. He might recognize me. He might fire me before we even got to the *Book of Knowledge*. And even if he didn't recognize me, he might get pretty sore about a junior trade writer attacking a cornerstone account, an institution.

"Couldn't we just get another writer?" I asked him. "Why bother Mr. Bernbach with this?"

John explained that I had made some very telling points and that Mr. Bernbach would want to hear them and find out if there was any truth in my observations, because this agency was very concerned with truth.

That afternoon Bernbach saw us. He looked at me without recognition and without interest, and his blue gaze became colder as John Blumenthal explained my problem.

I expanded on what John said, giving the example of *moon* and one or two other things Andy and I had tried to look up.

"I've got a set at home," Bernbach said. "I'll try these assignments tonight, and I'll see you here at ten in the morning."

I didn't sleep too well that night. Six weeks in Paradise had given me a taste for the place, and the thought of losing my job filled me with dread.

John and I showed up at ten o'clock. Bernbach sent his secretary for coffee for us, which I took to be a good sign.

"I did the assignments," he told us, "and all the information I looked for was there, but I don't think I could have done it if I were a child. You were right in refusing to work on the *Book*," he said to me. "I called them this morning to resign the account. The letter will go out today."

He sipped his coffee, enjoying the looks on our faces.

Lifting his cup in a toast, he said, "It's good to have you with us, and I think this was a very good way for us to meet."

I smiled happily and stroked my moustache.

I worked on everything I could get my hands on. I was Ray Ponterotto's favorite pinch hitter, filling in on booze, beer, shoes, candy, anything that came along. I got my first taste of television when Mary Wells asked me to cover a shoot for Paula Green, who was on a vacation. There was really nothing for me to do, she said, but it was an agency rule to have a writer on every TV shoot, just in case some last minute changes were needed. Mary let me know in no uncertain terms that she didn't want any last minute changes and that I was expected to just go and keep my mouth shut.

The shoot was for Salada Tea, and we were set up to do two sixty-second spots in one day in a studio on 10th Avenue in the 50s. They were both performance spots, with actors speaking throughout. These days, we usually shoot for two days to do one thirty-second spot of this kind, but back then, we were all still learning.

The first spot featured a Chinese actor in traditional costume, pouring tea and talking about tea as he moved around an elaborately designed oriental set. The actor spoke English quite well with a charming Chinese accent and a winning smile. The only wrong thing about him was that he couldn't act. And in order to say his lines clearly, he spoke with maddening deliberation. The spot was running about fifteen seconds over length, and the director yelled, "Writer!"

I couldn't see how to cut the script without completely rewriting it. I hated to do it because it was a beautifully written script that got in all the selling points with wit and elegance. I hated the idea of messing with Paula Green's words, and I hated more the idea of facing Mary Wells, who in her quiet way had managed to terrify me, with work she hadn't approved. But it seemed I had no choice.

I rewrote the thing, saving what goodies I could from the original, and called Mary to read her the result. Her secretary told me she was out for the day and she didn't know how to get hold of her.

I spent the rest of the day, which went on late into the night, in a cold sweat.

When we looked at the dailies the next day, Mary was furious.

When we looked at the rough cut a few days later with Paula, she wasn't too happy either. She didn't mind the rewrites (the second spot was seriously overlength, too), but she thought the acting and the direction were wooden and lousy. I felt miserable until Paula said, "I should have realized how slowly that

Chinese actor spoke, but I've got no excuse for the timing on the Boston spot. I guess my mind was on vacation. You did a great job. You can rewrite for me any time."

"The hell he can," Mary Wells said.

"Rita Selden is on vacation, and I hope you have time to fill in on Polaroid," Ray Ponterotto said.

I thanked him because Polaroid was a showcase for the agency, but told him I never again wanted to shoot anybody else's script.

Ray explained that this was brand new stuff that I would write and shoot, so I jumped at the chance. He handed me some work requisitions and told me to go see the account man, Joe Daly.

Daly was an ex-fighter pilot who looked every bit of it, except the *ex*. I wouldn't have been surprised to see gun mounts on his desk. Jack Dillon once described Joe as looking like a man who owned a fleet of steam shovels.

"You're not just filling in for Selden," he growled. "If you can write Polaroid commercials, it's your account. I've had it with her. We've had the account for seven years, and she's the ninth writer I've fired for it. Including Phyllis Robinson."

It was a nice first meeting—at least when I compare it with many meetings that followed.

Joe gave me a good briefing, telling me all the possible selling points for the camera and giving me a sheaf of his most favorite scripts to study. These days a stack of videocassettes would be the reference, but tape was another thing that hadn't been invented yet. The Polaroid spots were all broadcast live, not on film, because it was still necessary to prove in front of a live audience every night that the camera actually worked and delivered a good snapshot in a minute. The only visual reference for a live spot was a kinescope, which was made by pointing a movie camera at a TV screen, and these were only made on special occasions.

Before starting my first script I went to see Phyllis. She confirmed that Daly had fired her from the account and told me that he thought nobody but he understood Polaroid commercials and that he could write them better than anybody if he only had the time. She advised me to be, or at least act, as tough as Joe.

"Remember, he can't do you any harm. The worst he can do is throw you off the account, in which case you've joined a pretty good club."

The typical Polaroid commercial would start with Gary Moore saying something like "Hey, Carol Burnett, give me a smile; I want to take your picture. (SNAP) Now, folks, in sixty seconds . . ." Or maybe it was Steve Allen going into the audience and selecting someone. "What's your name? And where are your from? Brooklyn? (PAUSE FOR APPLAUSE) Okay, Brenda, smile for me (SNAP), and in sixty seconds I'll give you a great souvenir to take back to . . . where did you say you were from?"

The commercials always ended with a close-up of the picture being peeled off the backing and turned to the camera. And the audience always applauded. It was amazing.

I brought Joe my first script. Before he started to read it, he picked up a pencil and held it at ready over the copy. Well, I thought, this was a good time to start acting like a tough guy.

I leaned over the desk and took the pencil out of his hand.

"Let's get started right," I said. "If you want any changes made, just tell me and I'll make them. You run the account, but I run the pencil."

I thought for a moment that he was going to kill me. Then I knew that he only wanted to beat me senseless. Then, with a visible effort, he made himself speak calmly. "I'll let that pass because this is your first time with me. But don't fuck with me. Nobody can write these things—or rewrite them—as well as me. So give me back the pencil."

I handed him the pencil and took the script from his hand at the same time. "Here's your pencil," I said. "Write your own script with it. And if you find you can't do it, don't call me. Ask for writer number eleven." I walked out.

I was halfway down the corridor when he came out and yelled, "Get your ass back in here! I think I like your style."

Of course it wasn't my style he liked—it was his. I was only acting like Joe Daly.

I was asked to do an ad with Helmut Krone. I've forgotten what it was for, maybe for some pro bono thing like National Library Week, but I've never forgotten my first meeting with Helmut.

I'd heard a lot about him, of course; his work for Volkswagen and for Polaroid in magazine ads was already legendary. His brilliance was matched, everyone said, only by the thorniness of his personality.

When I told a couple of people that I was scheduled to work with Krone, they warned me to prepare for bluntness, rudeness, arrogance, intolerance, cruelty, and stubbornness, and to be prepared to deal with these for a long time, because Helmut was so intense about his work that he was the world's slowest art director.

Thus cheered, I went in to meet him.

Krone was a man of about thirty whose very German face featured strong bones barely concealed by a hint of plumpness. He wore a tan suit in a very conventional Ivy League natural-shoulder cut with a white shirt and a regimental tie. A small drawing table in the center of his bare white office was the only evidence that he was not an account executive.

I introduced myself, and he said a polite greeting in a manner that suggested he had memorized it for just such an occasion and was proud that he had remembered to say all the words.

I sat and said nothing. I had been told not to rush, not to make small talk, and not to take the lead. I looked at Helmut. He looked at the ceiling. Then he looked out of the window at a view of a nearby brick wall. I looked at the ceiling. Then I took my turn looking out of the window while Helmut gazed intently at the floor. This went on for a long time. I began to get nervous. Helmut appeared nerveless and quite at ease.

After more than half an hour of this, I began to get a little panicky. Maybe he was waiting for me to say something, to come up with an idea, a trial headline? After all, I was the writer, right? I started thinking in earnest about the ad, looking for some handle, some way to open up the conversation.

Another fifteen or twenty minutes of silence went by while I tried, and rejected, a series of ideas. Finally, at the point of desperation, I had one I thought might be worth a try.

I cleared my throat. "Um. I, uh, think I have an idea."
Helmut looked me in the eye for the first time. Then, very
deliberately, he said, "What's your hurry?"

We never completed that project. I spent three days with
Helmut, slowly getting to know a little about him. We talked
about architecture a lot; when he learned I had worked for
House & Home and *Architectural Forum,* he warmed up some
and started making sketches of the house he was building in the
wilds of Westchester County, near Katonah.

He was, of course, his own architect. "You know the Petite
Palais at Versailles?" he asked. "Well, it's going to be a small
contemporary version of that." As if that explained everything.

We talked about sailing too. He was fascinated by the idea
of it, and I drew diagrams to explain how a boat could sail into
the wind.

Once in a while, we talked about the ad we never did.

Finally, some work was demanded by Volkswagen, and Helmut had to give up the Library Week project. We parted in good
spirits with Helmut hoping that we would work together sometime on something real. I had actually enjoyed the experience of
three days with Krone, but now Polaroid and Joe Daly were
pressing me as hard as VW was pressing him.

Helmut's work style was only an exaggeration of the normal
work style at Doyle Dane Bernbach. Any given team of art director and copywriter spent a lot more time gabbing about sports,
politics, the weather, personal life, movies, theater, TV, gardening, books, music, hopes and dreams and fears than they did
talking about the ad they were supposed to be doing. But we all
got to know each other that way, and to know each other with
the peculiar sort of intimacy that lets long-married couples
speak in shorthand.

That intimacy always, or almost always, let us know when
it was time to get to work in earnest and just how to go about it.
"Okay," one would say, "what are we trying to say in this ad?"
And the other would say it, as simply and clearly as possible.
And then, suddenly, the ideas would start to emerge; and in an
hour or two the walls would be covered with rough tissue lay-

outs, most of them pretty good, a few of them better than that and, once in a great while, one of them just terrific.

The intimacy, the sort of private language, was department-wide. While we worked in teams, these were never exclusive relationships. A writer would work with one art director on one account, another on a second, and sometimes yet another on a third. This made for a team spirit that was, even then, recognized as a rare and wonderful thing. People were constantly looking in on other teams to see what kind of great stuff they were doing. Word of an exciting new campaign spread swiftly, and everyone would come in to see it. The best feeling in the world was when someone would interrupt your work and say, "I hear that you guys are doing great stuff. Can I see?"

We couldn't get enough of each other. We worked in teams, we ate in groups, and almost every week, some one of us gave a party. Parties were given by Judy Protas, Adrienne Claiborne, Ron Rosenfeld, Paula Green, Bob Levenson, Dick Rich, Ellen and me—everyone who wasn't a suburbanite.

Bob Levenson and I went to all of them, I think, because we made the music. Bob played the mandolin sweetly and accurately, and his job was to carry the tune. I played the twelve-string guitar, which I had more or less learned to play on my own, providing the strong rhythm, approximate harmonies, and a nice warm sound. My main job was singing, because I knew all the words, and Bob's melody line kept me from straying too far from the tune. We had the titles of some two hundred songs we knew typed on cards and stored in the spare string box of my guitar case.

Sometimes people would sing along, but mostly they just left us alone except to bring us drinks from time to time and to tell us we were sounding particularly good that night, which was never true.

And then, Monday morning when we went back to work, we had the feeling that the party had just started up again.

Polaroid was going really well. I started working with Bill Taubin on the print part of the account, doing full-page ads and the occasional spread to run in *Life* magazine. A spread in *Life*!

That, in 1959, was the big time, equaled only by having a four-color ad in *The New Yorker*. We did good ads; I got my first raise and with it a promotion to Copy Supervisor.

Copy Supervisor then, at DDB was pretty much the equivalent of what would later be called Group Head and is now called Creative Director. I could hardly believe this had happened. I had been at the agency for about six months, starting as a trade writer; and now I had my own group of accounts built on Polaroid, then the biggest account in the agency, spending some $6 million.

My other accounts were several brands of Schenley booze, Canadian V.O. being the best of them, an air-filter range hood that didn't need venting and was meant for apartment dwellers, ABC trade, Chemstrand Nylon fibers, Acrilan trade ads, and Buxton wallets. With the exception of Polaroid, this wasn't exactly a thrilling group of accounts and offered little promise of making anyone famous, but it was a group, and it was mine.

Awards were just starting to become important. At that time there were just two shows, the Art Directors Club and the American Institute of Graphic Arts (AIGA). The Art Directors Club was the big one, and it was important even for copywriters to get an award in the annual show, or even just to have an ad in the book. This was true even though the Club gave no recognition or credit to copywriters.

The awards shows were simply affairs, not black-tie dinner dances with speeches and entertainment like today's extravaganzas. The Andys, Addys, Clios, One Show Awards, Gold Lions, and $100,000 Kelly prizes were undreamed of, much less the dozens of regional events around the country.

I didn't even go to the first show where I won some awards. I don't know if anyone at DDB did. I don't know where it was held, what went on, or anything else about it. All I know for sure was that I won some prizes for Polaroid print, Acrilan trade, Chemstrand, and, wonder of wonders, a first prize for Best Live TV Commercial. Of course this was easier than it sounds because the live TV spot was rapidly becoming a thing of the past and there was little competition for Polaroid.

The awards didn't make us feel special or superior. We felt that already, just for being at DDB, but they were a pleasant acknowledgment of our superiority. How good we felt about ourselves! It was not only that we knew we were bright and witty and talented, but that we also knew the way, had the formula, for making advertising the public took to its heart.

It was so simple we wondered why it wasn't being done in every agency for nearly every client. The basic disciplines were the same as those used at any professional ad agency: find a motivating proposition to put before the right audience and say it clearly. But we went a couple of steps past that. We added to it the idea of word/picture integration, the conviction that the audience was intelligent and had a sense of humor, and finally a horror of ever doing anything that had been done before.

When I think of how we felt about ourselves, there is one moment that captures it best for me. Bill Bernbach decided to show the Creative Department the agency's new business presentation, so we would understand how he was selling our talents. He invited us to have coffee and Danish at the Persian Room at the Plaza Hotel, with the presentation to follow.

During the coffee period I chatted for a while with Dave Reider, who was then Copy Chief of the agency. Dave was a quiet, serious man whose delightful sense of humor was rarely shown except in ad copy. He was by nature a grave person, a sort of Jewish Abe Lincoln, I used to think, or maybe a James Stewart.

Dave said in his most earnest manner, "I think that every time in history has a group of individuals who best capture the spirit of that time, like Shakespeare and Johnson and Marlowe at the Mermaid Tavern, or the Algonquin Round Table group—Dorothy Parker, Alexander Woolcott, F. P. Adams—for the 30s. I think for now, it's us."

As the 60s dawned, we were all to become famous, as Andy Warhol said, for fifteen minutes. How many of our names will even the most ardent fan of the Creative Revolution recognize today?

We were Sue Brock, Stan Burkoff, Adrienne Claiborne, Jack Dillon, Ken Duskin, Les Feldman, Margaret Fishback, Bob

Gage, Monte Ghertler, Bernie Gilwit, Paula Green, Frank Kirk, Helmut Krone, David Larson, Bob Levenson, Leon Meadow, Sid Meyers, Bob Olsen, Lore Parker, Charlie Picarillo, Judy Protas, Dave Reider, Dick Rich, Phyllis Robinson, Ron Rosenfeld, Sam Scali, Rita Seldon, Len Sirowitz, Ben Spiegel, Fred Stadelman, Burt Steinhauser, Bill Taubin, and Mary Wells.

That list yielded three agencies still in business, three members of the Copywriters Hall of Fame and three members of the Art Directors Hall of Fame, and the names still on agency doors plus a very few others, are those you might know. But at the time, almost every one of us felt touched by glamour, sprinkled with star dust, and destined for greatness.

◆ ◆ ◆

Every copywriter and art director in the business wanted to be one of us. We had our pick of the best talents of the day, and as we grew we hired them.

Well, most of them.

Somehow we missed out on Ed McCabe, one of the greatest of copywriters, who still says his one disappointment in life was not having worked at Doyle Dane Bernbach.

I don't know how that happened, but I do know how we missed out on Jerry Della Femina. It was my fault. I reviewed his sample book three times during the course of two years, and three times I turned him down.

The trouble with Jerry's work was that he wrote brilliant, arresting headlines that had little or nothing to do with the product. These headlines usually painted him into a corner that he couldn't get out of, so it looked like he didn't know how to write body copy. I thought he was smart, talented, erratic, unsound, and wrong-headed and would go nowhere in the business.

Win a few, lose a few.

Years later, when Jerry was rich and famous, I saw him standing alone at a Herb Lubalin Roast at the Art Directors Club. We had never met during the times I had turned him down; I had only seen his book. I left the table to go to him.

"Hello," I said. "I'm David Herzbrun."

"I recognized you," Jerry said. "I was going to go over to introduce myself, but I was afraid you'd reject me."

I had been hired in 1959 for $13,000 a year. By 1961 I had been given two raises and was earning $18,000. This was enough for a large three-bedroom apartment in Riverdale with a sweeping view of the Hudson, a sporty Sunbeam Talbot convertible, membership in a swim and tennis club in Westchester, and a maid who came in twice a week.

Other agencies paid better, and DDB writers and art directors were often wooed by them, but nobody left. After all, it wasn't as if any of us was going hungry, and we knew that our creative egos would never be so well fed as at DDB.

That was the problem I talked over on the phone with Bob Gill, a designer I knew who had moved to London. He called me at home to ask for my help in finding a "DDB-type" copywriter who would like to move to London. Bob was a consultant to an ad agency there, and since he was an American, they had enlisted his help in this search.

London sounded fascinating, but the pay sounded awful. It amounted to only $12,000. Gill assured me that this was equal to almost twice the amount in New York, in terms of buying power. Evidence that it was high pay was the fact that the writer was wanted to be the creative director of the agency (the title had finally been invented) and that the compensation would include some perks, a practice unheard of in New York, such as a company car and membership in "a decent club."

I told Gill that I'd nose around and see if I could find anybody smart enough to do the job and dumb enough to leave Paradise for less money at an unknown agency in a chilly, wet climate.

I put down the phone and went back to finish breakfast and tell Ellen about the call. It was a Saturday, so we had plenty of time to discuss the allure of living in London, a city we had never seen. Of course, like all heavy readers of fiction, we thought we knew all about the place, and we were slightly Anglophilic as well.

The more we talked, the more attractive the proposition looked. If I could get Bernbach to give me a leave of absence for, say, three years, it could be a great adventure for us and for Andy and Douglas, our ten-year-old daughter and five-year-old son.

We discussed Ellen's pregnancy, and she said the move was okay with her. They did have doctors in England, she said, and if she wasn't happy with them and missed her own, she would simply fly home a week or so before she was due.

I wasn't really surprised by her reaction. Ellen has always been as impulsive as I from the day I met her, which was the day I proposed marriage and the day she accepted.

Even if Gill was exaggerating and our living conditions would turn out to be a lot less than we were used to, it could be really exciting. Vacations in France, Italy, Scandinavia occupied our fantasies. Weekend jaunts to Cornwall, to Wales, to sailing waters of the Norfolk Broads all seemed immensely seductive.

I called Gill the next morning and asked whether he thought I'd be right for the job, and if so, I'd be interested.

INNOCENTS ABROAD

I saw Bill Bernbach first thing on Monday morning. I told him that I didn't want to leave DDB, but that the opportunity to live in Europe was a rare and exciting one and would no doubt contribute to my growth, both personal and professional. I asked for a three-year leave of absence.

Bill turned me down. He said that he simply couldn't guarantee that there would be a job opening when I came back. All he could promise me was that he would hire me without question if there was a need.

I told him I'd think it over again.

The next day I told him that I had decided to take my chances and had accepted the job. I gave him four-months' notice, firstly because it would take some time to arrange for working papers and to organize the move and secondly because I was in the process of getting Polaroid to agree to make a produced, filmed TV commercial and wanted to finish the project.

It was time to go beyond the live spots. Viewers all believed by then that the camera worked, but they weren't so sure that they wanted one. It still seemed like a gadget. If we shot commercials that showed people using the camera and having a good time sharing the pictures right away, we might convince the audience that a Polaroid camera did more than simply record good times; it actually made the good times better.

Taubin and I put together a lot of storyboards for spots showing families, lovers, old couples with grandchildren, people on farms, in cities, at a zoo, at a country fair—warm, heartstring tuggers. The only copy in each spot was a question: "If Polaroid had been invented first, would there ever have been another kind of camera?"

We never produced these spots, though they were the starting point for the great campaign created by Phyllis Robinson and Bob Gage, as they got the client softened up and interested in doing warm commercials about the camera's contribution to an experience, and not about selling hardware.

We didn't go on with the campaign because life took a sudden new direction for me that removed me from the Polaroid account and from the dream of living in London in a little mews house just across from a grand old local pub.

"We've decided to open an agency in Germany, in Düsseldorf," Bernbach said. "If you haven't signed a contract with the London agency and if you'd like to go live in Europe and stay with DDB too, I'll send you over as Creative Director. How about it?"

I said that it sounded wonderful, but I'd have to talk it over with my wife. Bill suggested that I call her right away, from his office.

Ellen listened and then said, "When do we pack?"

Bill said that he planned to send an art director and an account man to work with me and suggested I talk to Paul Wollman, an art director who had only recently joined the agency. Paul was not as yet deeply involved with any account, he explained, and if I thought I could work with him, I should ask him if he'd consider the job. As for the account man, they hadn't, as yet, figured out who they could spare.

I knew Wollman slightly. We had done an ad together, and we had had lunch a couple of times. He was a cheerful man with a sharp wit and a lovely way with a conversation. I had no idea of whether or not he was a good enough art director to found and run a department, especially in a foreign country where neither of us could speak the language, but he had to be pretty good to have been hired at DDB. And language wasn't going to be his problem; it was going to be mine.

I didn't know how we would work. I presumed that Paul and I would do an ad; I would write it and have it translated and hope that the translator had some style, as well as accuracy.

Paul was fascinated by the idea. He, too, had never been to Europe, and it sounded exciting and challenging to him. "But Germany," he said. "Does it have to be Germany? Do you think we can live with people who slaughtered our relatives? Could we ever get it out of our minds?"

I said that I was prepared to try it, that if we were ever to teach the Germans new and better values and bring them back into the human race, we would only do it by mingling with them, not by isolating them. For us, the great mass medium of advertising was a perfect platform; we could use it as a civilizing force.

We went to lunch and talked some more. It was clear that living and working in a culture we didn't understand and a language we might learn but would never master was not going to be easy. On the other hand, Germany would be virgin territory for the kind of advertising we did. We would be all alone, bringing a fresh, contemporary look to the work, being human, warm, humorous, irreverent, and brash. It was chancy, but it brought with it the opportunity to change the way a whole nation thought about advertising.

I felt it was irresistible. Paul said he'd talk to his wife.

Paul and I went to Germany for a tour of the Volkswagen factory. We flew to Hamburg, where we stayed for a night at the Vier Jahreszeiten Hotel to meet and talk with Ned Doyle and Ed Russell.

We found them, an unlikely couple, nearly lost in the vastness of a couch, surrounded by old mahogany tables and huge lamps and overhung with a floral bouquet suitable for the marriage, or death, of an emperor. Doyle, a leprechaun in a strange land, was sipping his usual Chivas Regal with lemon twist; and, as usual, the bottle stood on a table near at hand. Russell, a tall, slim young man, was busy acquiring continental (or at least German) airs with an iced glass of Steinhager. He ordered some for Paul and me, saying that we would have to learn to develop a taste for it; it was the In Drink in Germany today. I have always believed that if Russell were to wake up in some strange place where he had never been, say a village in rural Nepal, he would not only know exactly how to behave but would have the right clothing in his bag. Russell was the top account man on VW in the United States, and he would be in charge if we were able to get the account in Germany. He and Doyle told us what the situation was, and it sounded a little less than promising. Volkswagen had no ad agency in Germany, but did their own work out of an advertising department of some 135 people. These writers, art directors, designers, photographers, and print production people turned out all the catalogs, brochures, posters, displays, and other showroom material needed. They also created and placed one ad a year.

Just one ad, and it ran just once.

Dr. Hahn, the Ad Director, a former member of the Nazi propaganda ministry who had worked closely with Dr. Goebbels, discouraged any advice from any VW agency. He protected his empire jealously.

As for the single ad, it was little more than a statement of the number of VW Beetles, bus-style station wagons, and Kharmann Ghias the factory had built in the preceding year. It was placed in every publication in Germany, regardless of editorial content. The ad ran in general magazines, business publications, newspapers, trade journals, comic books, scholarly quarterlies, porn rags, fashion magazines, satirical monthlies, college literary and humor magazines and yearbooks, women's club and fraternal organization annuals, theater and opera and sports programs—everywhere, in short, where Dr. Hahn could buy space.

His theory was that all publications are corrupt, and if one wanted good publicity from them, one had to pay for it with advertising. Furthermore, VW as an enterprise largely owned by the government could play no favorites.

As for running the ad only once, the arithmetic was clear. If you bought a page in every publication, the cost came to 20 million Deutschmarks, or $5 million, and that was exactly VW's advertising budget for the year in Germany.

Our job, Doyle and Russell told us over lunch at the Vier Jahreszeiten, was to create great advertising for the German market that they could present to Dr. Nordhoff, the top man at Volkswagen and Dr. Hahn's boss. If the ads really excited Nordhoff, there was a chance that he might order Hahn to hire us, or even fire Hahn.

Sure thing, we said. Piece of cake, we said, while our heads were still reeling and our bodies dully aching from our first jet lag.

We napped until dinner, and after that were shown the fleshpots of Hamburg, the famed Reeperbahn. A few drinks deceived us into thinking we'd gotten over our jet lag. Doyle knew his way from bar to bar in any city in Europe, and Russell was learning fast. We learned only one thing: English is spoken by the doorman-cum-barkers, bartenders, waitresses, and hookers at only the very worst places.

The morning added hangover to jet lag, and in a grey, chilly drizzle we set off for Wolfsburg, called by Germans "the town without a past."

Wolfsburg looked like an architect's rendering of a planned town. All the lines were too straight, and the bare little trees that lined the wide boulevards looked like sketches. Children played, like mechanical toys, in the sterile, architect-designed playgrounds. There were almost no people in the streets. All of the cars parked by the curbs or driving in the sparse traffic were Volkswagens.

We were taken to the Guest House, the first building of any age we had seen in the district. It was a pleasant building that had once been a small hotel, and its exterior had some character. Inside, it was cold and bleak with bare, scrubbed wood floors, an uninviting barroom, and a dining room that was evocative of boarding schools. We were checked in to small cells, dropped our bags, and met in the bar.

Lunch was across the street in what was Volkswagen's equivalent of a senior officers' club—a warm, cozy, comfortably furnished lounge. We were introduced to Dr. Hahn and his assistant, Helmut Maasen. Both spoke excellent English.

Hahn looked much as we thought he would: a strong, dark man in his early fifties with a formal aspect and a firm handshake. His greeting, neither cordial nor chilly, was a perfect display of good manners. Maasen's greeting was much less formal, almost American. He was a lean man with a handsome, witty face, and he smiled easily.

We had an assortment of cold cuts for lunch: sausages, cooked hams and raw hams, liverwurst and blood sausage, with potato salad, green salad, and a basket of bread and rolls, all washed down by the best beer I had ever tasted.

While we ate, Hahn questioned us. How did we expect to make advertising in Germany when we didn't speak the language? We told him that original and strong selling ideas were seldom about language and would surely translate.

"Umm. Perhaps," he said doubtfully. "But how can you create original and strong selling ideas for a people whose culture you will probably never understand?"

We answered that our very lack of understanding would probably keep us from advertising cliches, would certainly lead us into unusual ways of thinking and of expressing our thoughts, and if we made mistakes and came up with occasional ideas that nobody understood, our clients would certainly stop them from running.

"Hmm." He was more than ever doubtful, and he decided to change the conversation. "Your names," he said, "Herzbrun and Wollman; these are very German names. Herzbrun is fountain of the heart, and Wollman is wool man, or wool merchant. But I have seen how you spell them. In Germany, each would end with a second letter *n*. How is this?"

Paul answered. "We're Jews," he said, "and it's our tradition to cut off a bit of our endings."

"And how do sales for the fourth quarter look in the states?" Maasen hurriedly asked Russell, and Hahn joined the new conversation with relief.

We toured the factory for all the next day, taking notes about steps in manufacture and assembly that might make good selling points in ads. We ended the day with a dinner and a cheerful, long night of drinking with Maasen and Russell.

The next day, Russell returned to Hamburg en route to New

York while Paul and I took the train to Düsseldorf. The landscape was flat and boring, and the day was, like the preceding two days, chilly and grey with occasional rain. An English-speaking waiter in the dining car seemed surprised by some offhand comments we made about the weather, with hopes that it would clear for the weekend.

"Clear for the weekend? You are making a joke?"

When we assured him we were only voicing a hope from first-time visitors who wanted to spend a pleasant weekend in Düsseldorf, he laughed as if we had in fact made a joke.

"I can promise you a clear weekend," he said, "maybe in April but certainly in May. It happens every year with no fail." He walked off chuckling like S. Z. "Cuddles" Sakall.

Düsseldorf was not as pretty as Hamburg. The buildings that lined the Königsallee, the great central boulevard, were new and graceless. In the sixteen years since the city had been flattened by field artillery, there had been time to clear away rubble and build a new city, but no time or money for architectural aesthetics.

The rain fell steadily, making a million rings in the green canal in the strip-like park that ran down the center of the Königsallee. The trees were black with wetness. We checked our bags at the elegant Breidenbacher Hof and, following directions, walked a few blocks to the offices of Von Holzschuher & Bauer, the agency that DDB had bought a majority interest in.

We met the Baron von Holzschuher first. He was a tall, heavyset man with a full mane of flowing white hair. When we sat, I noticed that his feet were surprisingly small and delicately shod in patent leather evening pumps. Startlingly, he wore women's sheer silk stockings. The walls of his office presented a gallery of black and white photographs of beautiful women; there were at least twenty of them.

The Baron noticed that I was studying them. "My ex-secretaries," he explained. I said that I'd sure like to meet his present one. "Of course, when you visit in my office in Munich. I always keep my secretary in Munich."

Dr. Bauer, who was in charge of the Düsseldorf office, was quite the opposite of the flamboyant Baron. He was an affable, unpretentious man dressed in tweeds who welcomed us with an offer of coffee and expressions of his pleasure in meeting us and his eagerness to start work with us.

Over coffee he said that he understood part of our reason for spending a few days in town was to get started looking for living quarters. To help us he had taken the liberty of hiring a secretary for us and was sure that we would find her to be all we wanted. Her name was Birgit Jacobsen, and she had full secretarial skills, including shorthand, in German, English, and French. "She is ready to take you for a tour of the city now," he said. "Would you like to get started?"

Birgit came in, a slim, dark, good-looking girl who greeted us with a bright smile, a firm handshake, and flawless, British-accented English.

We broke our first German business rule by following the Baron's lead and taking our secretary to lunch.

In the next few days, with Birgit's help, we found what we were looking for. Paul, who owned a house on Long Island, rented a modern apartment on the top floor of a slick new six-story building in the fashionable Zoo District, where there is no Zoo. I, who was an apartment dweller, rented a generous town house with three floors and a garden in Oberkassel on the bank of the Rhine opposite Düsseldorf. It was almost considered suburban.

We flew home to start work on the easy matter of turning out some VW advertising good enough to make Dr. Nordhoff cry out in ecstasy.

A Volkswagen Beetle looked just the same in Germany as it did in the United States, but in advertising and marketing terms, it was a completely different car. In the United States, a Volkswagen was small, cheap, cute, funny-looking, and anti-establishment, while in Germany it was oversized, high-priced, boring, middle-class, and old-fashioned. As for its appearance, it was far from funny-looking; 40 percent of all the cars on the

German roads were Beetles. The large municipal parking lots were so full of them, in every color, that they looked like trays of Easter eggs.

Our problem was to find a way to keep up the cocky, brash tone of the American Volkswagen advertising for this dull, conventional car.

The first ad we did, after wrestling for a week or ten days with the job, looked just like most of the American VW ads. It showed a noncommital photograph of the car in limbo, in black and white. Under it was a headline that read, "It isn't cheap to buy, insure, or maintain. So what makes it such a bargain?"

I had hardly any idea of how to write the copy that would be the answer to that question, but luckily I didn't have to. First, VW had to buy the agency, then they had to buy the ad, and those events were a long time off.

We did perhaps a half a dozen ads that Bernbach liked. Then Ed Russell asked us if we could do a few TV storyboards, just to show Nordhoff that we were good at doing them and that we could handle the standard German time of thirty seconds.

Thirty seconds? How could you do a TV commercial in thirty seconds? How could you in that brief time attract a viewer's attention, get him involved with your story, make a selling point, and leave the scene with a smart, pointed little joke as a reward for paying attention?

That was how TV spots were made. And the standard length in the United States was sixty seconds, which always seemed a little too tight.

Russell said that he couldn't tell us how to do it, but was sure we'd find a way. We asked for examples that had been done in the U.S. market, but he told us that stations and networks had never sold thirty seconds, so there was no precedent. We'd just have to invent the form.

To make it worse, he then told us how TV commercials were seen in German broadcasting. They were grouped in blocks of from five to fifteen minutes of nothing but commercials. To stand out and be remembered in this clutter of ten to thirty spots would be a wonderful challenge, he said.

We wrestled with the wonderful challenge for almost a month. When we were done, we had five storyboards to show to

Bill Bernbach. He loved them all, which was a rarity and a great source of pride.

Of those initial five spots, one would become the most famous commercial ever shown in the United States (though it was first run in Germany). Another of them, never shown in the United States, was to become the most famous spot ever in the history of German advertising. Its tag line, credited to me and Paul, is in *Geflugelte Worte* (it means "winged words"), which is the German *Bartlett's Familiar Quotations*. So familiar are the words that the book does not explain that they are from a VW commercial, because who wouldn't know that? Yet all they say is, ". . . goes and goes and goes . . ."

Of the three other spots, two won nice awards in European competitions, and the third was a complete disaster.

All in all, not a bad month's work.

We had planned on leaving for Germany in March, because it was going to take that long to get our apartments ready. Paul's wasn't quite finished, and our house needed complete redecorating. Jack Lane, our third member, who would be in charge of account management, had just agreed to go and hadn't even found a place to live.

We were not happy, therefore, when we were told in mid-November that we had to be in Germany with our families before January 1, in order to meet some German tax law's requirements. We explained that our homes wouldn't be ready, and even if we were willing to camp out, it would be a long time before our furniture came.

"Don't even think about it," said Dorothy Parisi, DDB's Office Manager, who had been put in charge of our German move. "We're not going to send your furniture anyway. You'll buy what you need there. In the meantime, while the stuff is on order and your apartments are being fixed up, we'll put you up in a hotel."

The three of us had our doubts about living in a hotel for a couple of months with two kids to each family, but Dorothy swept those aside. She had been assured by Joachim Schurholz, our German lawyer, that we were greatly overstating the amount of time it would take to get us set and that we'd be out of the hotel in a matter of weeks. There was no arguing with Dorothy, who had the heart, soul, and manner of a marine drill sergeant. We barely had time to pack things for storage or to ship clothes and such personal stuff as books, records, and a few paintings. We were put on a plane, all twelve of us, snugly jammed into economy class seats, to arrive in Düsseldorf on December 30, 1961.

◆ ◆ ◆

We settled into a whole wing of the little Münch Hotel, on the Königsallee just a couple of blocks away from our offices. Each family had two rooms, one for the adults and one for the kids, plus a seventh room that was used as a community TV room and playroom. The children ate at a table set up in the hall that served these rooms. Since the Münch Hotel had only a breakfast room, dinners were brought in by frock-coated waiters from a restaurant next door and served from silver dome-covered platters to the unimpressed kids, whose ages ranged from three to ten.

We adults ate all of our meals at restaurants, all three couples always taking dinner together. We did this for more than three months, an amazing thing for people who had never met until a couple of weeks before our flight from the United States.

During these months, it was a relief for us to have a job to do and an office to go to. We had a client, our very first, who had been convinced by Doyle and Russell that we could work wonders for his Hamburg-based coffee business. Marx Herz, founder and boss of Tchibo Kaffee, had built a huge business and in the process had created one of Germany's biggest ad budgets. It became major news in the German ad trade press, and even *Der Spiegel,* Germany's *Time,* that Herz had appointed an American agency run by three New Yorkers who couldn't speak German.

Well, I had been studying German, as intensively as I could, for the last couple of months. I had been busy translating the lyrics of Brecht's *Three-Penny Opera* for training, and I had been reading, dictionary at hand, as much as I could manage of *Der Spiegel* and a couple of other magazines. It wasn't much, but it was enough for me to judge that the translations Birgit did for us were stiff and formal, not breezy and slangy. Birgit agreed and said, after all, she wasn't a writer. If I wanted style, I should hire a copywriter whose English was good enough to have him understand what I wanted.

I hired Claus Harden. His colloquial English was American accented. He was a student and fan of DDB advertising in the United States and was thrilled to be our first employee in the embryonic Creative Department.

Paul and I created the ads for Tchibo Kaffee. Then we would have Claus look at the rough layout and the headline and tell us whether it would work in German. If his answer was yes, I then wrote the copy and handed it to Claus to put into German.

It didn't take long for him to complain. "This isn't going to work," he said. "If you wanted a translator, why did you hire a copywriter?" He was right, of course, so we found a new way to work. Paul and I still conceived the ad and had Claus check out the headline, and then I would tell Claus what the copy was supposed to say and tell him to write the story his own way. The only caveat was that he would have to take me through his copy word for word and idiom for idiom so that I would understand what it said.

The first time we did this I was puzzled and depressed by the formal structure of his writing, the long sentences, the lack of punch. "That's not how we write," I told him. "I want writing that's like the way people talk. Incomplete sentences. One-word sentences. One-word paragraphs, even. You know what American DDB advertising is like. Let's do the same in German."

"We can't do it," Claus said sadly. He explained that German is really two languages: the oral and the written. There are words and entire cases that are never spoken, only written. And there are others that are good spoken German but that never appear on a page except as dialogue. And as for incomplete sentences and one-word paragraphs, well, that just wasn't German, even if people did speak that way.

I didn't care whether it was good German or not. If people spoke that way, then I wanted our ads written that way.

Claus looked upset. "But David," he said, "if I do that and if Max Herz is crazy enough to accept it, people will laugh at us and think we are ignorant and uncultivated. We'll be the laughing stock of Germany, and we will both lose our jobs."

I told him that if he did what I asked and he was right, it would be at least three months before the ad ran, another month for us to become a laughing stock, one month more for Bernbach to find out about it, and another month before we were fired. That was a good six months of safety. On the other hand, if he refused to do what I asked, I would fire him immediately.

He smiled, told me I was crazy, and an hour later came back with a piece of copy that seemed just right to me.

Meanwhile, Paul was having a problem trying to find a photographer to shoot the Tchibo ads. We'd thought that Germany, home of Leica and of Zeiss lenses, would be populated by good photographers, but that was as dumb as assuming that, because some of the world's best cookware comes from Germany, it must also be the home of some of the world's best cooks.

German photography was about as heavy and unimaginative as German cooking.

I kept Paul company as we visited photographers in Düsseldorf, Hamburg, Frankfurt, which was the center of advertising in Germany, and even as far as Munich, where we visited with the Baron.

The Baron had us out to his home on a lake outside of the city, which had a nice view of one of Mad King Ludwig's castles on the far shore. Then he took us to town to tour Nymphenburg Palace where he showed us Ludwig's Gallery of Beauty, a whole museum filled with nothing but paintings of his many mistresses. We began to understand the photos of the Baron's secretaries that lined his office walls.

Nowhere did we find a photographer who worked as Paul wanted, with natural light. They all had windowless, skylightless studios filled with every kind of artificial lighting. Everywhere we went we made contact with local agency art directors and asked them if there was a photographer anywhere in Germany who liked to work with daylight. We began to hear about one, Charles Wilp, who lived and worked in Düsseldorf, but we were assured that we wouldn't want to work with him because he was crazy.

We arranged a visit and found Charles to be a thin, mop-headed man who looked like Marcel Marceau out of makeup. He and his partner, Ilse Dwinger, a big and handsome blonde woman, greeted us warmly in excellent English and showed us the studio with pride. It was a sort of greenhouse that Charles had built on top of an office building. The roof and three walls were glass. Behind the fourth wall was a darkroom, a tiny kitchen, and a bath. Ilse and Charles also lived there, sleeping on a mattress on the floor.

There wasn't a light in the place, not even in the kitchen or the bath, except for the red light in the darkroom. Charles was so fanatical about natural, available light that he rose with the first dawn, and when there was no more light for work or reading, he sat on the mattress and listened to music by the light of the city around him.

Paul asked if we could see some of his work. All Charles showed us was a series of large black and white prints of light. No subject matter, just a background of white no-seam paper hanging to the floor or curving on to it, shot at different times of the day and under different skies. A few were relieved by having a sort of buckling area of the paper, as if it had been blown forward on one side by a breeze. They were oddly fascinating and very, very strange.

When we asked to see some commercial samples, Charles explained sadly that he had yet to be given his first commercial assignment. All he had done for a living prior to this was photojournalism. He had done it well for some while as a staffer for Paris *Match* and for years as a free lance, and he had made enough money to build this little gem of a daylight studio. But then he found that no German art director wanted to work with daylight. He was broke and would probably go back to journalism unless something came along in the next month.

We thanked him for showing us his work and promised to keep him in mind when an assignment came up.

"What do you think?" Paul asked as we walked back to the office. "Do we take a chance on him?"

I said that unless we were under some heavy deadline, there was no risk in trying Charles. If he couldn't give us what we wanted, we could give up and take the job to one of the better hacks we had met.

The next day we gave Charles our first Tchibo coffee ad to shoot. It showed a hand rejecting a coffee bean with a flick of the finger that sent it towards the edge of the page. It wasn't an easy shot, but Charles did it beautifully.

With the publication of this ad and with the others that quickly followed, Charles Wilp's fortunes were reversed. He began getting work from other agencies, and people in other agencies began to talk about Paul and me.

We also began to get more business.

In June of 1962 our third child was born. We named her Jane Emily. We hired a new housemaid, trained in child care, who spoke no English and could not pronounce *Jane*. It came out "Yahneh," a sound we didn't like. I remembered, from doing my Brecht translations, that the prototypical Anglo name among Germans was Jenny, which was closer to Jane than was "Yahneh."

Now, twenty seven years later, she is still Jenny: one small permanent effect on our lives of our German adventure.

With the addition of Hanne, our new nursemaid/housemaid, our household staff now consisted of three people. The other two were Frau Jaspers, who did heavy cleaning, and Herr Jaspers, who came in twice a day, seven days a week, to care for our coal furnace; shoveled snow in season; and kept the rose garden in good trim.

All this, plus three floors of a town house and a late model Mercedes in the garage, on a salary of $18,000 a year.

It was a good time to be in Germany.

TV commercial time was scarce and usually had to be bought a year or more in advance, but Max Herz somehow was able to buy some for Tchibo, and we hurriedly created some storyboards. He approved them but turned down our request to work with an English film production company. We felt we'd have a lot more control if we could communicate easily with the director, but Herz said that film production was very good right there in Hamburg and that we would have to learn to work in Germany sooner or later.

When we reviewed the show reels of the Hamburg film production houses, we again asked Herz to let us work with better talent, but he suddenly became very patriotically German, and we had no choice but to pick the best of a bad lot.

The results looked just like the work of the still photographers we had seen before Charles, except that they moved. A little. The actors were the kind you put back in the box at night. The director was playing the part of an Obersturmbahnführer in the SS. The sets, to give them their due, certainly looked like sets, and the lighting was surely a work of art, because it in no way resembled anything that occurred in nature.

Max Herz agreed with us and promised that next time we could work with any director we wanted. They don't make clients like that any more. We never worked again with a German film company, for Tchibo or any other client.

Suddenly we were the hottest agency in Europe, and it seemed to happen all at once. Our client roster got bigger every week or two. Volkswagen gave in and hired us; and before our first year was out, we were working for a linoleum company, a venetian blind company, a cigarette maker, a sanitary napkin and tampon firm, and more. These were all German companies, not local offshoots of business DDB had in New York. We did get some of that sort of work, too, including Polaroid, but it gave us very little satisfaction since the work was created in New York, and we were just there to translate it and run it.

When Volkswagen gave us approval to shoot three spots, they did not include the two that later became classics. They didn't actually kill those, but put them aside for a while. They were a little nervous, had never done TV before, and wanted to do the spots that had more linear logic.

We asked to be allowed to work with English film production houses.

They asked us to use German firms.

We said politely, but firmly, that we would do so if ordered, but would take no responsibility for the finished commercials.

They thought for a while and then responded that we could use French film makers if we wanted, but not English. This decision was based neither on aesthetics nor politics, but had something to do with currency exchange rates and the Common Market, of which Great Britain was not a member. We agreed.

We had already seen some good French commercial reels and weren't at all bothered by the idea of shooting in Paris for a couple of weeks.

And then we learned about working with the French.

The commercial is very simple and very graphic. It starts with a metal bucket, into which water is dripping. We pan down on the bucket to see that it has rusted through and water is leaking from it. We then pull back and see a large block of ice fall into the bucket. The pullback continues until we see the faucet, at the top of the screen, which has been leaking. A hand turns it on full. The water is hot, and when it hits the ice, it steams up. Steam fills the screen as we dissolve to a front view of a Volkswagen. We move in to a close-up of the windshield, as the washers squirt and the wipers start working. The End.

The copy to be read with this says, "The trouble with water. It rusts metal. When it's cold, it freezes. When it's hot, it boils over. That's why we don't use any water in our car. Well, hardly any."

The trouble began, as sometimes happens, with the storyboard. Paul had drawn it so that in one frame we see the ice starting to fall toward the bucket, and in the next we see it resting in the bucket, broken into two pieces. "This scene," said the French producer, "could present some problems, but our effects man, he is very clever and surely he will find a way. You are not to worry."

We were puzzled about what the problem could be and why we would need an effects man.

"To break the ice, so to speak, that will be uneasy."

We told him that it wasn't necessary, that Paul had just drawn it that way to give some sense of drama to the storyboard. The real drama would come just from having a block of ice fall from nowhere and drop noisily onto our bucket.

"No, no" the producer said, "the broken ice, it's a stroke of genius, very beautiful; we will not give it up, never. You are not to worry."

Well, we decided, if they could do it, it might be nice at that.

A couple of weeks later we drove to Paris with our wives, full of high spirits and anticipation, and checked into a little hotel on the left bank, the Claud Bernard, that Birgit had recommended. The producer and the director took us for an excellent dinner; and by the time we had finished it, with a great deal of wine and a few cognacs, we knew we were going to be lifelong pals.

The next day, we showed up on the set at a little studio out past the Bois de Bologne. What we saw was quite strange. The bucket was on a table, and over it was a heavy scaffold where two men were struggling to secure a block of ice in the jaws of a giant C-clamp. Each time they thought they had it, the ice would melt a little and start to slip out of the clamp.

We asked why they were doing that.

The director pointed to the frame in the storyboard that showed the ice starting to fall. "Here," he said. "This scene starts so, with the ice suspended over the pail."

We explained that there was no separate scene, that the action was to be continuous from the start to the steam, but somehow failed to make him understand or, if he did understand, failed to get him to agree.

I suggested that he forget the clamp and just put the ice on the scaffold and, on cue, have a man drop it into the bucket.

"No, no!" cried the producer. "It's too *dangereuse*! We must have the clamp. Please, you will just sit there and have a coffee, and we will make it work. I promise."

We sat there and had a few coffees while they messed around, drilled some holes in the ice, modified the clamp's grips and its quick-release mechanism, and rehearsed a few times.

Meanwhile, we looked at the lighting. It was dominated by a curious rig neither of us had ever seen before. It was a large board, about eight feet square, that was covered with light bulbs of 100 watts each set in rows about six inches apart. If those measurements are correct, there were some 200 bulbs. The board was covered in foil to reflect as many of the 20,000 watts as possible.

It was weird, but when we looked through the camera, the lighting was just fine. We began to feel a little more confidence.

The director called for a full rehearsal, with camera running just in case everything worked and the timing was right. We went to our canvas chairs to watch. *"Les lumieres!"* called the director. Then, *"Camera!"* and at last *"L'action!"*

The assistant director then started a countdown. *"Dix! Neuf! Huit! Sept! Six!"* and I noticed that he was looking across the studio and holding up his hand to signal someone. I located the someone. It was the effects man, bent over a plunger-style detonator.

"Cinq! Quatre!"

I followed the fine wires leading from the detonator. They led to our block of ice.

"Trois! Deux!"

"Get down!" I said to Paul as I dropped to the floor and pulled him with me, just in time to hear *"Zero!"* and the explosion of the ice and the nearly simultaneous explosions of dozens of light bulbs that had been hit by flying ice.

Paul was bleeding from a small ice wound in his forehead. I had been hit on the shoulder by a chunk, but was unhurt. All I could do was to lie on the floor and laugh and yell, "Print it! Print it! I've got to have that as a souvenir!"

Of course the French were offended that we thought them clownish. That made them sullen and even more stubborn than the French usually are. While they abandoned the dynamite and agreed to give up on the broken ice, we couldn't talk them out of the giant clamp. They shot all day and were never able to keep the action on time.

The next day, more sullen than before, they agreed to try it our way. It worked, and we were done by day's end. There was no wrap party because the production company had lost money on the job and decided to blame us.

The next two spots we shot in Paris, with two other production companies, were just as confused, though not as memorable as "The Day the Ice Exploded." One spot had to be reshot, and the other needed to be reshot twice.

Now there were two countries we would never film in again.

Doyle Dane Bernbach GmbH, Düsseldorf, was growing rapidly, with no help and no little hindrance from Von Holzschuher & Bauer. DDB severed the relationship, and we moved out of Grünstrasse to a five-story building of our own in Schadowstrasse. We scarcely had time to wonder what we were going to do with all that space when we began to fill it.

It was against the law in Germany to approach an employee of a company with a job offer because manpower was in short supply, due to the war. For the same reason, it was almost impossible to find an unemployed person to approach, especially if you were looking for a talented copywriter or art director.

Okay, I'll confess. The statute of limitations probably doesn't run twenty-seven years, even in Germany, and they most likely can't extradite me for solicitation.

We hired Dick Calderhead away from Y & R in Frankfurt. Dick was a bright, talented American art director who thought about advertising the way we did, and it was great to have another one of us there.

We hired Ursula Roos from Y & R, too. Uschi was a cute and funny German gamine who, at twenty four years old, had already worked in New York, Rome, and Paris. She was fluent in English, French, and Italian, plus Dutch. She could curse filthily and with conviction in all her languages. Uschi was also a terrific art director whose main strength lay in creating campaign concepts.

Writers were harder to find. Most were still mired in literary German, and the few who were trying to imitate our new style were doing it with a clumsy self-consciousness. New York sent first aid in the form of Alan Mond, who was at best a mixed blessing.

Alan was a barrel-chested, powerful young man with big hands that he used expressively when he talked—or when he became quarrelsome, which was not an uncommon occurrence. He could be, in his frequent manic moments, a hilarious storyteller and stand-up comic. In his equally frequent depressive times, long and silent broods would be ended in sudden eruptions of rage during which he might put his fist through a wall.

There was no question about Alan's talent, but his immediate distaste for Germany, which grew into a sometimes near-violent hatred for the country and all its people, did get in the way of his work.

Sometimes, though, it actually worked for him.

A great example is the Mum deodorant campaign. When we were given this assignment, we were doing more than introducing Mum to Germany; we were introducing the idea of a deodorant.

With the exception of a small fraction of the population—sophisticates, world travelers—Germans didn't use deodorant. They also didn't wash or clean their clothes very often. (An average German in 1962 wore a business shirt five times before washing it and had his suits cleaned only twice a year.) So, even though Germans were very fond of baths and showers, they did tend to smell rank. Very few Americans could handle the smell of a crowded German place, such as a department store, the first few times they tried to shop. The odd thing is that you could eventually get used to the smell and, finally, not notice it.

This fact was going to make it awfully hard to sell Mum.

The Germans, of course, didn't notice that they smelled bad. How could they? They had been smelling that ripe odor all their lives.

Alan, working with a fine German designer/art director

named Rainer Lubke, went right for the throat. Or the armpit. Their first ad was a small portrait of a beautiful young woman, delicately framed in a hair-line rule and centered in the page. The headline below it, in an elegant, romantic script, read, "She stinks."

The second ad played on the envy with which German women viewed American women, whom they believed all to be fabulously spoiled. Its headline asked, "What do German women have that American women don't?"

Even hostility can be made to work for you.

Tchibo's claim to superiority was that they bought their coffee beans directly from the growers in the best coffee growing regions around the world. They often contracted for entire crops before they had been picked, rather than be forced to buy commodity coffee on the open market.

To illustrate this, we created a TV character, the Tchibo Coffee Expert, whom we would show buying coffee in Kenya, checking the roasting in the plant, dropping in on a store for a quality control check, and so forth. This time we won the right to shoot with an English company.

We had been in Germany for more than a year and had never been to London. We had no idea of which film companies to see or even how to get started. I phoned Ronnie Dickenson of Collett Dickenson Pierce, a bright, creative agency that had an informal cooperative relationship with DDB New York (CDP handled Polaroid and Chemstrand in Great Britain and kept their campaigns consistent with DDB's in the States). I asked him for advice and counsel.

He gave better than that. He said that he would have his secretary program a week of meetings and screenings for us. We set a date two weeks off and started looking forward to it as if it were to be a holiday. Our wives were wild with excitement at the prospect of being able to shop in English, to see a play perhaps, maybe go to a night club, all things that our German was not yet up to.

London was a revelation. It was sunny and mild, not bleak

and chilly. Its buildings were cream colored, not sooty grey as we had imagined them. The names of streets were familiar to us, the signs on the shops were in English, we could talk to the cabby and the desk clerk!

Ellen and Ann went shopping; Paul and I went to meet Ronnie Dickenson. He and his Creative Director, Colin Millwood, took us on a tour of the agency. A long wall was completely covered with familiar ads from Doyle Dane Bernbach. A sign on the wall invited staffers to take down one of these ads and replace it with one of their own any time they felt they had earned the right. On close examination, we saw three or four ads that were CDP's work. They looked perfectly at home with the display.

We were introduced around the Creative Department where everyone treated us like movie stars. They were terrifically excited by our presence in Europe, even knew some of our German work, and every one of them asked when we were planning to open up in London.

Dickenson's secretary sent us on our way. Our first visit was with a company called Film Contracts where we met and had lunch with Leon Clore and John Arnold. As we were parting, Clore said casually that there was to be a cocktail party that evening at a club on Curzon Street and that a lot of advertising people would be there. Would we like to come? Bring our wives, of course. Well, of course we would.

We saw two more film companies that afternoon, then went back to the hotel and told Ellen and Ann about the party. What a chance to wear the new things they had just bought!

The party was large, noisy, and cheerful, filling a suite of white and gold rooms. We met creative directors, writers, and art directors from a dozen agencies, all of whom asked when we were planning to open up in London. We went on to dinner with a group and then to some private club after for drinks.

It wasn't until two in the morning when we learned that the party had been given by Leon Clore and that it had been in our honor.

And that's how the rest of the week went.

Suddenly, we were celebrities, in Germany and in London, in Paris and in Amsterdam. At least we were celebrities among advertising people.

I once wrote that I had become world-famous, but that very few people were aware of the fact.

At home in Düsseldorf, the growing community of Pop Artists accepted advertising as one of the Pop Arts and treated us as fellow artists. Pop Art was new, and one of the few European galleries that would handle it was owned by a Düsseldorfer named Schmiele. Because of him, the city had become a center of international Pop Artists.

Charles Wilp took them all in, bought their work, and even built a private gallery for it. He gave receptions and parties for each new artist to arrive in town.

The group, all quite unknown, included Christo, who wrapped things; Yves Klein, who painted solid blue canvases; Tinguely, who made motor-driven sculptures out of wires and bits of metal; and Armand, who exploded objects and mounted the results. (I particularly remember a violin that had had a small charge set off inside it.)

Christo had not as yet wrapped a building, a canyon, or an island. In those days he wrapped obscure objects in burlap and twine and displayed them on framed boards. Sometimes the shape hinted at what had been wrapped, but only marginally.

One night Christo staged a "happening" at a party. He talked a girl we knew, named Brigitte Wolfe, into letting him wrap her in the nude in clear plastic. Because she was quite a beautiful girl with a remarkable body, we all paid close attention as Christo helped her out of her clothes as if he were unwrapping a gift package and then began to wrap her as Charles took pictures and the stereo blasted out Fats Domino music.

I guess I was the only one to take time out to look at her face. Her head was covered in clear plastic, she looked frightened and about ready to faint, and her color was slightly blue.

I pushed through and told Christo to unwrap her head, but he only looked puzzled that anyone would interrupt him in the midst of creating.

I think it was Dick Calderhead who cut open the plastic with his pen knife while I grabbed Uschi to get her to phone the hospital to send the paramedics.

We couldn't find the phone in its usual place. Then I noticed its wires running up the wall into an ambiguous framed Christo artwork that could only be the phone. I began to untie the twine that held the burlap in place when Charles grabbed it from me and hugged it protectively.

"You're ruining it!" he said.

"He's killing Brigitte," I answered.

"Without art, what use is life?" Charles said grandly.

Calderhead and I worked on the introduction of a new cigarette.

We visited the factory in Berlin and saw how cigarettes were made. We thought we might do an interesting campaign on the selection and trimming of the tobacco leaves, the curing process, the kind of filter material that was chosen, and so on. We speculated that it would be a refreshing change from the typical lifestyle cigarette campaign and that it would at least give smokers a reason to try the brand.

The cigarette was named Bremen, for reasons we could not fathom.

Dick designed a handsome red package with a graphic representation of a cigarette with a cork tip making a white stripe down the center of the panel. Then we started making ads.

We did, in fact, build a campaign on tobacco leaves and process. And we wrote what may be the weirdest claim ever made for any product: "Maybe you'll like them, maybe you won't."

The slogan implied, of course, that Bremen was noticeably different from other cigarettes, and the client assured us that the final blend would be. Unfortunately the product was bland and totally without distinction. The distinctive advertising should have had a product to fit it.

As the campaign broke, the Surgeon General of the United States declared that he had determined that cigarettes were hazardous to health and must carry a warning. He added that advertising of cigarettes should be banned. The advertising trade press went wild, and every major figure in the agency business was interviewed on the subject.

Ad Age had asked Bernbach what he thought about it, and Bill had replied that he was pleased to have no cigarette business and would never take any. The savvy *Ad Age* reporter reminded him that we had just broken our new campaign for Bremen. "Well, that's just in Germany," Bill said.

As soon as the story came out, Doyle phoned us with instructions to resign the business before the client could read that Bernbach apparently didn't mind poisoning Germans.

The launch of the brand was a fabulous success, followed by swift decline and failure. Every smoker tried Bremen and decided there was nothing much to like. Except, maybe, the ads.

The British army school that Andy and Doug were attending stopped teaching kids at age eleven, when most British children are sent away to boarding school.

Andy passed her "eleven-plus" exam with high grades, indicating that she should go to a good "public school" (we call them private schools) in England. After touring a few recommended institutions, we selected the Grove School in Hindhead, a town about an hour's drive south of London.

We missed her a great deal; the family was fractionated and incomplete. We went with her six-year-old brother Doug to visit her as often as possible. Andy quickly learned to speak upscale English English. Doug, with his repertoire of American, British army cockney, and foul-mouthed guttersnipe German, was appalled. His sister had become a class enemy. And at home in Düsseldorf, little Jenny was beginning to speak, but only German. Hanne would not let Doug speak German to her unless he cleaned up his act.

We were becoming a rather odd family.

In the early spring of 1963 we finally got approval to shoot the one commercial we most wanted produced out of the first group we had created for Volkswagen before leaving New York. It was a spot that answered a question nobody had ever asked: How does a snowplow driver get to the snowplow?

We hired Leon Clore's Film Contracts to shoot the commercial. John Morris was the Producer, John Arnold the Director. They set about finding some place in Europe where there was still snow, other than the inaccessible peaks of the Alps. They finally located an area of high Alpine meadows near St. Cergue, straight up from Geneva.

We decided to shoot with two cars, one prepared for export with American market signal lights, bumpers, and trim and fitted with Michigan license plates that we had made in our studio. We were that sure that when the people at Volkswagen of America saw the spot, they would want one for use in the United States.

There was not enough snow at St. Cergue. Worse, there was not a road that hadn't been perfectly plowed all winter long. We created our own roads by driving the car parallel to lines of utility poles that crossed open fields. Each location we found could only be used for one take, because each called for trackless roads. We moved our cars and crew throughout the district, shooting for a full week, shivering in the icy fog.

We edited in London; and when we saw the dailies, our hearts sank. The lack of snow was obvious. The locations were so varied that there was no hope of matching the light of one scene with the next. Focus was crisp in some scenes, soft in others. The thing was going to be a disaster.

You know what happened next.

"Snowplow" took top honors at the Cannes Film Festival, the American Film Festival, and in every show in Europe, London, and the United States. Nobody ever noticed how imperfectly it was filmed, not even the people at the Museum of Modern Art in New York, who selected it as the first TV commercial to be included in their permanent film collection.

I mentioned this years later to a woman in the museum's film department. She told me that I must never confuse art with technique and pointed out that if the museum did that, it would be filled with Rockwells and own no Picassos.

I learned from "Snowplow" that art, at least the performing art that is advertising, is always about ideas and seldom about technique. I have never seen a great idea ruined by poor production, and I have never seen a bad idea saved by great production.

I have often made this point when young creative people have insisted that their commercial will be destroyed if not shot by one of the star directors of the day, usually in London. I have made these teams look at "Snowplow" carefully, to see all of its flaws.

They never see them. I have never made my point.

So much for "The Art of Persuasion."

By the end of 1963 we had been in Germany for two years. We had built a successful business, had a staff of over one hundred people, and had established that DDB's kind of advertising could cross cultural and linguistic lines.

In those two years, the three of us had not gotten a home leave, nor even a business visit back to the home office. We had also not been given a raise. We decided to speak to Bernbach about it when he next came to Düsseldorf. It was a conversation we didn't look forward to with much pleasure or confidence.

We talked about it over dinner early in 1964. Bill was surprised to hear that we had not had a raise and promised to do something about it promptly. As for the home leave, we told him that other Americans working abroad for other American agencies got full family leaves of a month every eighteen months on average. And it wasn't counted as vacation time. Visiting one's family was viewed as a necessity, but not as a vacation. He was interested to learn of this and promised to take it up with Doyle and Dane and Dorothy Parisi.

As we walked from the restaurant to the hotel, Bernbach told us what a great job we had done and promised us that we would share in the fortunes of the office as soon as it was in the black. "You'll all be making enough money so you can bring your family home any time you want, at your own expense. You'll do very well with us."

His mood was so warm and expansive, none of us wanted to

break it by pointing out that our German operation had been in the black for nearly a year.

A week after this conversation, Joachim Schurholz, now our Managing Director, told us that Bernbach had instructed him to raise us each by 8,000 Deutschmarks a year, which amounted to $2,000. That would have been a nice annual raise for a copywriter or an art director or account executive at home. But it was an insulting amount for two years' work by people in responsible management positions who had to deal with a foreign culture and language and to build an agency from scratch all at once.

Being the writer, I was elected to write a letter telling Bernbach our feelings. I made it direct and simple, neither pleading nor demanding. Instead of hearing from Bill, I got a furious phone call from Doyle, telling me that he was grabbing the next plane to come settle our mutiny.

Well, he and Bernbach eventually simmered down. We all got raises of $3,000 more, which we felt was enough. But things were never quite the same again between DDB's management and me.

A few months later, when things had gotten back to normal in our relationships with Bernbach, the bottom dropped out of our world. From our mail pouch from New York, we each received a prospectus that told about DDB going public. We read it carefully. It was a fait accompli, not an invitation to participate in some coming event.

We reviewed the list of people who had been sold stock prior to the issue, and we computed how much money they had made overnight. People with far less responsibility than each of us had—Copy Supervisors, Art Supervisors, Account Supervisors—had been rewarded for their work, but not us.

Nobody got rich on that public issue except the principals, but even a modest amount like $100,000 looked to us like a lot of money, and we were shocked that we had not been included in the handing out of largesse.

Since I was already in Bernbach's doghouse, I volunteered to make the call.

When I asked him why we had not been included in the stock distribution, he seemed puzzled by the question. "But I'm sure you were," he said. "you certainly deserved it, too."

I told him that we could find our names nowhere in the prospectus, and he said he'd look into it right away and get back to us within an hour. When he did, it was with apologies and genuine regret. He explained that when he, Doyle, and Dane had decided who would get how much, they reviewed the complete list of employees and, of course, we were not on that list, and we were simply forgotten. Worse, it was irrevocable. Now that DDB was a public company, there could be no more sales of stock at the low pre-issue price. But he would find some way to make it up to us.

We asked why our names were "of course not on that list," and Bill said that it was a list of employees of Doyle Dane Bernbach, Inc., and we were employees of a German corporation.

It was the first we'd heard of that, too.

Work went on. Paul and I kept churning out Volkswagen ads at the rate of a dozen a year. Some were pretty good. Only one hit the jackpot with the perfect inseparable marriage of word and picture we always sought to create. It was the rear view of a VW Beetle drawn in black marker on an egg, so that the egg looked like the body of the car. The headline read, "There are some shapes you can't improve."

We were spending more time in London, both producing TV and starting to lay the groundwork for a London office, due to open by the end of the year. We were in London often enough to make it economical to rent a large furnished maisonette, an apartment with a three-level split plan, in fashionable Cadogan Place overlooking the Gardens.

We began searching for office space, looking all over London. Unlike New York, there was no central district where agencies clustered. We narrowed the search to the district between Baker Street and Regent's Park, for reasons I have forgotten. When we had two or three spaces that looked right to us, Dorothy Parisi came to make a final selection and sign a lease.

We took a set of offices on three floors of a fusty, dark, old building in Baker Street, moved in, and started hiring a skeleton staff, including a secretary and a TV producer, Vickie Saunders, who would help Paul and me with our growing workload in London.

Our wives began looking for places to live in London. We figured on getting replacements for ourselves in Germany at the end of our third year abroad.

One Saturday in Düsseldorf, Paul and I found it necessary to work. We met at the coffee shop in the ground floor of our building, together with a secretary who had volunteered. After coffee, we let outselves into the building. To do this, we needed a key to the street door, a key to the inner door, a key to open the elevator, another key to operate the elevator, a key to the Art Department floor's elevator door, and a key to the door from the elevator lobby to the inner corridor. We had the full set.

When we had opened the last door, we found that a pair of doors halfway down the corridor, which we had never seen shut, had been shut and locked, barring us from Paul's office. None of our keys fit.

We phoned Schurholz, who would have the key, but there was no answer.

We phoned everyone we could think of who might have the key, but it was a rare day, sunny and warm, and nobody was staying at home in such weather.

Our secretary tried every locksmith in town, but none was open.

She tried the police, but they declined to come pick our lock, no matter what identification we could produce.

The doors were wood frames with panels of wire-mesh glass.

Each had a pushbar. Paul and I each grabbed a pushbar, and we rocked the doors to try to break open the lock. We couldn't do it, but there was a slight splintering sound for encouragement.

"Maybe if we kick it like cops do in movies it might open," I said.

"Give it a try," Paul said.

I braced myself for a good, hard kick, and as I unleashed it, I lost my footing, and I kicked through the wired-glass panel instead.

I knew right away that I had severed my Achilles tendon.

I spent a month in the hospital, with members of the staff constantly coming in to show me work. I was on the phone with Bernbach or Ed Russell or Doyle in New York at least once a day. As I was nearing release from the hospital, Bernbach called to tell me that he wanted me back in New York instead of going to London to live.

I protested, but it was no use. He and everyone else in the New York office had come to the conclusion that I had broken the door in a fit of uncontrollable temper, that I had cracked under the strain of the last three years, and that I was too unstable a personality to entrust with the responsibilities of the London office.

PUTTING MY BOOK TOGETHER

I returned to New York feeling cheated, mistreated, and misunderstood.

My first day in the office didn't make it any better. I was told to go to personnel to fill in all the usual forms that a new employee has to deal with.

I was given one for the profit sharing plan, and I said that I was already a member of the plan. The personnel person told me that I had been dropped from the plan when I left the employ of the company to work for a German corporation and that I would have to go through the two-year qualifying period again and then start vesting at the rate of 20 percent a year. That meant that in the five years I had worked for DDB, I had built nothing so far and would build nothing until my eighth year.

I also learned that the pension plan was now closed to new employees, though it was to be continued for those already in it. I had been in it, but was not any longer.

In short, I had nothing to tie me to the company. There were no reasons, either financial or emotional, for me to keep working there. There was only one compelling reason for me to say.

There was no possibility of getting a good job with the sample book I had to show. Everything in English was more than three years out of date. Nobody would know how to deal with the German work, except for "Snowplow," and I would have trouble showing that because it had just taken top honors in New York with an American cut and copy credited to Bob Levenson and Len Sirowitz, who had worked on the adaptation.

I had to work long enough to build a new, exciting book that would get me out of DDB.

Bernbach was shocked to learn about the profit sharing and pension plans and promised to see if anything could be done about them. As with the stock, it was irreversible.

I told him that if he was looking for a way to make it up to me, the best way would be to give me a lot of accounts so I could prove to him what I was worth.

He assigned me to Avis, Chivas Regal, Jamaica Tourist Board, and Thom McAn. They were fine accounts, but all of them had already won big awards in the last year, and they didn't look like they offered me a way to make a name for myself. I asked for a piece of new business when it came in, and Bill agreed.

I worked on Avis with Helmut Krone. It was slow, often painful process, but ultimately tremendously rewarding. Helmut was the best reader and critic of copy I have ever known. When I would bring in a piece for him to review, he would take his time, become completely absorbed in it, and then usually put his finger on one word or phase that seemed wrong to him.

"Avis doesn't talk like that," he would say.

He was always right.

We tried to define how it was that Avis talked, and we finally worked it out. It was like Broderick Crawford in *Letter to Three Wives*. It was the voice of a successful man who was very intelligent but not well educated and who had been raised on the wrong side of the tracks.

This made it a lot easier to write Avis ads. It also gave me a new tool that I started using on every piece of business I had. Before writing, I would first either cast or create the character who was to do the writing. This allowed me to write in a distinctive and appropriate style for each campaign. These characters became so real to me that even today, more than twenty years later, I can recall each of them vividly: the Scottish-born, English-educated New Yorker who spoke for Chivas; the Jamaican sugar millionaire whose English family had settled on the island four centuries ago and who had studied literature at Princeton; the ex-army Platoon Sergeant from Newark, New Jersey, who spent a lot of time on his feet in his appliance store and who thought a lot about shoes. I am sure that I could still write in each one's tone of voice, remember each one's vocabulary, and construct a paragraph in the distinctive rhythm of each one's speech.

I have created new characters and sometimes recycled some of the old ones for all the campaigns I have done since them. I've also suggested the technique to many young writers, and it has been a boon to them all.

It took an art director to think of it.

Doing Avis was a joy because I not only had a great art director in Helmut Krone, but a great client in Bob Townsend. Townsend had taste and guts; he was willing to take chances, and he trusted us completely. Only once did we have a serious difference of opinion about an ad.

Helmut and I had rented an Avis car to drive out to see Townsend at Avis World Headquarters on Long Island. When we opened the ashtray, we were really upset to see it jammed up with butts. We had been promising clean ashtrays in our ads, and our current outdoor billboard, which we passed on the way, read, "Avis won't rent you a dirty car. No ifs, ands, or butts."

"We have to do an ad on this," Helmut said. I put the butts into an envelope, at his suggestion, and we started working on what we wanted to say in the ad.

We got it done a couple of days later. It showed the envelope spilling butts onto the page. The headline read, "The writer of this ad rented an Avis car recently. Here's what I found."

The copy began by saying "I write Avis ads for a living, but that doesn't make me a paid liar." The last line read, "They'll probably never run this ad."

When Townsend saw it, he was appalled. "You're not serious about wanting to run this, are you?" he said.

We assured him we were. The ad, we said, would show the public that Avis was really as honest as our other ads had been saying they were.

Townsend said that it went against everything he believed about how to do advertising. It was negative. It kept on being negative. And as for its style, it wasn't Avis. It was written in the first person.

"Right," we said. "And we want to run it."

Only a great client could have done what Townsend did next. He offered what he called a compromise. "I'll let you run the ad," he said, "on only one condition. You see to it that my secretary knows exactly where and when it's going to appear for as long as it runs, and she can see to it that I never see it again."

I worked with Burt Steinhauser on Chivas Regal. Burt was a tall, handsome fashion plate, a nonstop talker, a bonfire of enthusiasm, the complete antithesis of Helmut.

Bob Levenson said, "When you work with Steinhauser, somehow the room is always full of feathers."

His wall was covered with Chivas ads from the last two years. They were great work, starting with the first: "What idiot changed the Chivas Regal bottle?"

I complimented him on the work. He thanked me but added that there was one thing wrong with what he had done. Each ad was terrific, but there wasn't a campaign. He hoped that he and I could create a campaign.

"You mean a slogan?" I asked warily. DDB avoided slogans.

Burt said that no, he didn't mean a slogan, but an attitude and a look. I agreed, and we set to work.

The attitude that eventually emerged was based on the fact that the Scotch drinking public already believed that Chivas was the very best, plus the fact that it only cost $2 a bottle more than ordinary Scotches. Therefore, if you weren't serving Chivas, you were a stingy cheapskate.

The first ad we did had to be hurried out to make closing dates for the Christmas season of 1964. It had only a picture of a bottle of Chivas and the headline: "Go ahead, spend the extra $2. It's Christmas, isn't it?"

(The same ad ran again twenty years later, but with the $2 figure replaced by the word *money*.)

To get a new, consistent look for the campaign, Burt decided to always shoot the bottle so that we appeared to be looking down at it from about a 45 degree angle, to use a strong shadow, and to eliminate the backgrounds so that we always saw things against a pure white page. We also agreed to visually contain everything on the page, that is, not to have a hand holding the bottle, which would mean cutting off the arm by the edge of the page.

"Won't all that be awfully restricting?" I asked.

"Sure," Burt said. "But restrictions are what force us into new solutions. Restrictions always shove you into creativity."

From the very beginning with Aaron Burns, Herb Lubalin, and Lou Dorfsman, art directors have been among my best teachers. And even when I've been a little dull, they've made me look so good.

I had really looked forward to working with Bob Gage on the Jamaica tourism account. Bob was already a legend, DDB's first art director and a cofounder of the agency, who had set the strong graphic standards of the place. I went in to see him and tell him I was his new writer. He seemed pleased, but said that we would not be working together, in fact. He had already designed the landmark campaign, with its oversized JAMAICA crowding off the top and edges of the page, and he felt that he had little to do with creating subsequent ads. My real partner would be Dennis Stock, the photographer. Bob wanted me to work with him as if he were my art director.

We met the next day in Bob's office, and the three of us discussed what sort of picture stories we might want to look for on our upcoming trip to Jamaica. Bob's direction was wonderfully liberating. We were to shoot any picture that interested Dennis, whether or not I could see any immediate use for it. Dennis, in turn, was to try to make the best possible picture to go with any story I found that I wanted to write about. When we came back home, Bob and I would review the results and see what elements fit together to make the best possible ads.

I spent the next two weeks reading everything I could find about Jamaica. Dennis did an enormous amount of research on what had already been photographed, just to get a feeling for the place. We met at his house in Connecticut to look at the pictures and to plan our trip. Neither of us had ever been to the island, and we were very excited.

We stayed in Jamaica for two weeks, searching and shooting. I spent a lot of time in the Jamaica Institute, reading historical documents that might provide us with ideas for stories. That's how we thought of these ads, as stories, either photojournalism or historical yarns or romances.

I was in the Institute, reading about Port Royal, "the wickedest city in the world," that had one day slid into the sea and vanished with all its pirates, thieves, and whores. One note caught my imagination. It said that the Jews of Port Royal, while willing to live and do business in that sinkhole of sin, were unwilling to be buried there. They took their dead in black hearse-boats and rowed from the peninsula across Kingston Harbor to bury them in less unholy ground.

What a find! If that cemetary still existed, it would be the oldest Jewish memorial in the western hemisphere, a real tourist attraction for the substantial market of Jewish vacationers.

Dennis and I visisted the synagogue in Kingston and asked the rabbi, an elderly Englishman in a clerical collar, about the old cemetery. He had never heard of it. He showed us the graveyard behind the synagogue, and while it had some old and very interesting stones, they were not old enough by nearly a century.

I went back to the Institute and looked at ancient maps. I reasoned that if Jews then were anything like Jews now, they wouldn't have been terrific rowers and would have picked the closest place on the mainland for their cemetery. I marked an area a little to the west of Kingston, and Dennis and I set out in a car to find it.

It wasn't an easy coast to follow. There were lots of little peninsulas, each with a road down the middle and occasional paths off it to the shore areas. We stopped here and there and asked about an old Jewish cemetery, but nobody could help us.

Going down one of these peninsulas on a narrow dirt road, we found ourselves in a Rastafarian village. We had been warned to stay away from the Rastas, who were antiwhite and generally antisocial, and who, it was said, made their livings by stealing. We locked the doors and rolled up the windows and drove slowly, looking for a place to turn around. The road ended in the center of the village in a shabby little square. As I was starting to maneuver the car around to get us out, a crowd of people, all with their hair in dreadlocks, surrounded the car so that I could not move without running into someone. We stopped and waited, afraid of what would come next. The least that would happen, we told each other, was the loss of our money and passports and Dennis's cameras. We just hoped they wouldn't feel it was *de rigeur* to beat us up, too.

The crowd parted to let a tall man through. He wore a long robe and a lot of chains and medallions and carried a sort of shepherd's crook. There was no doubt that this was The Boss.

"You're the word guy," Dennis said. "You talk to him."

We both got out, and I started to explain that we hadn't meant to disturb their village, that we were looking for an old Jewish cemetery, that it was a kind of religious pilgrimage, and so on; but he wasn't buying it.

Dennis said, "Let me try something."

He dug into a pocket in his camera case and took out a large gold coin, which he handed to the Head Man.

"You're trying to bribe him?" I whispered.

"Shh. Let's see if this works."

The Rasta studied the coin, turned it over, and studied it some more. He then said, "You Dennis Stock?"

Dennis said yes, and when the big guy asked him for proof, he took his passport from the camera case and handed it over. The Rastafarian looked at the passport, handed it and the coin back to Dennis, and told everybody to go home and leave us alone. Then he told some kids to lead us to the old cemetery, shook hands with Dennis—but not with me—and walked away.

"What the hell is that coin?" I asked as we followed the kids down a jungle track. Dennis passed it to me.

It was a commemorative coin with a head of Haile Selassie on one side. On the other side was engraved, "To my good friend Dennis Stock from His Royal Highness, The Lion of Judah."

"I remembered that the Rastafarians think Selassie is God," Dennis explained.

"So you had this made up just in case?" I asked incredulously.

"Oh no. I always carry it. It's my good luck piece," he said. "Selassie gave it to me after I spent a few months in Addis Ababa doing a picture story for *Look* magazine."

It was the only time I'd ever seen a good luck piece work.

The cemetery was right where I had predicted it would be. The graves were large sarcophagi that had originally been about three feet high. Now, most had sunk below the level of the spongy ground, with only a few at grade level or slightly above it.

We cut away vines and overhanging shrubs to read the inscriptions, which were in three languages. The centers of the stones were incised in Hebrew, and around the outer borders ran Portugese. In an inner border was English.

Many of the stones carried one or another of two symbols that neither Dennis nor I had ever seen before, and I have never seen since. One was a straightforward piece of graphic communication: a sapling being felled by an axe-wielding, disembodied arm. It was on many graves of children and of young men and women. The other symbol was eerily cryptic and frightening. It was a screaming head gripped at its neck by a disembodied arm (the same diety?). Below the fist we could see the ragged edge of the neck, depicting a head that had been torn from its body. Nothing in the ages or the sexes of the deceased could help explain this dreadful icon.

Dennis took some pictures. I took some notes. Despite the humid tropic weather, I felt a chill. We left as soon as we could. The children who had led us to this melancholy place had fled as soon as they had led us there, but it was easy to find our way back to the Rastafarian village.

Our presence went unacknowledged.

We drove away without looking back.

Of course we never did an ad to send Jewish tourists to this dangerously situated shrine. But we did find the place fascinating. Anyone interested in learning more can read an article I wrote for the Jamaica Institute, in partial repayment of a growing debt of gratitude, or in the archives of the synagogue in Jamaica.

The first new account to come in was, as Bill had promised, assigned to me. It was Broxodent, an electric toothbrush. Helmut was to be my art director, and he looked at the gadget with distrust.

"I think it's dishonest," he said.

Bernbach convinced him that while you could certainly brush your teeth just as well by hand, this thing would be wonderful stimulation for the gums. Bill was big on stimulating the gums; he credited the Water Pik with saving his teeth.

Helmut listened and then agreed to work on Broxodent.

We spent the next couple of weeks playing with it. Helmut got a pane of glass and some toothpaste and doodled on the glass with the vibrating brush. There was an idea there, but we weren't sure what.

We did a two-page spread headlined, "Who needs it?" and answered the question in the copy. Another spread read, "Man vs. Machine," and its visual was one of Helmut's toothpaste-on-glass patterns showing the path of Broxodent versus the track of a regular toothbrush.

We made this into a sixty-second TV commercial, showing that it takes a minute to brush your teeth 200 times by hand, but that a Broxodent can do it in about three seconds. With the demo finished, the viewer was faced with about twenty seconds of watching and hearing nothing but a toothbrush making toothpaste marks on his screen.

It seemed endless, but for some reason hard to explain, it also seemed very funny.

It is oddly possible to bore people into laughter. The Volkswagen commercial that found its way into the German *Familiar Quotations* was a deliberate attempt to do this. It opens on the rear view of a Beetle as a man comes into frame, gets in the car, and drives straight away from the camera. The car becomes a speck and disappears in about fifteen seconds. For the rest of the commercial there's nothing to look at. All you can do is listen to the voice, which says, "There's a lot to be said for the Volkswagen, but the best is that it goes. And goes. And goes . . . and goes . . . and goes . . . and goes . . . and goes . . . and goes . . . and goes . . . and goes . . . and goes . . . ."

That's only fifteen seconds worth. The spot was thirty seconds long on air, but we made a sixty-second version for cinema showing. I've seen audiences react to it often, and it's amazing. At about fifteen seconds they get restless, waiting for something to happen. At about twenty seconds they know that nothing will happen. At about twenty-five seconds, they laugh; and at thirty seconds, they applaud. Then, as the thing goes on and on, the laughter builds and builds, like a kid being tickled and begging you to stop doing it. The message is inescapable: This commercial will go on forever, just like the car.

It's a nice piece of audience psychology, but I don't think it can be used very often. Maybe only once per viewing generation per country.

With five accounts, both TV and print, consumer and trade, I was pretty busy, but I could still hardly get enough work. I was, you remember, trying to build my book so that I could find a good job somewhere else.

I was having a wonderful time, but I could never get out of my mind how I had been treated. The matters of the stock, the profit-sharing plan, the pension and, maybe most of all, the judgment that I was incompetent to go on to live and work in London, all rankled and galled. I had to move on as soon as I could.

Just to have more samples to show, I started doing Dansk Designs ads free-lance with Lou Dorfsman, working nights and weekends.

It was one busy year.

In the Art Directors Club show for that year (Andys, Addys, Clios, and the One Show still hadn't been invented), I won nineteen awards, one or more for each of my five DDB accounts, plus one for Dansk.

I finally had my book together, and it was literally a book.

It was the *Annual* of the show, with index tabs on the pages that showed my work. I figured that would do the job.

The morning after the show, the headhunters started to phone.

CONFESSIONS OF AN OGILVY MAN

The only approach that interested me was from David Ogilvy. He was, along with Bill Bernbach, the other creative force of the time. Next to DDB's, Ogilvy's work seemed very conservative and visually rooted in old traditions, but it was always elegantly written and finished, always based on strong selling ideas and often memorable.

Ogilvy took me to lunch at a dining club high up in an office tower, driving me there in the company Rolls. Its license plates were OBM, as the agency was still called Ogilvy Benson & Mather. We sat in a private dining room at the club and started to talk.

We didn't actually talk; we chatted. We chatted about the advertising business, about travel and living in Europe, about favorite restaurants in Paris, about books and authors and theater in London and New York. The talk didn't once touch on the subject of my coming to work at OBM.

I found David to be an inordinately attractive man, not merely for his handsome, rosy-cheeked face, but for his manner, a curious mixture of academic and theatrical styles. He would have made a splendid Henry Higgins. He did in fact make a splendid luncheon companion.

Finally over coffee, Ogilvy said, "I suppose you'll want some good reasons for coming to work for me."

I was so charmed by the man that I said, "Just one good reason, and you've got me."

"One *good* reason," he said unhesitatingly, "is that I don't believe you can make Doyle Dane Bernbach a better agency than it is."

"And you think I can do that for Ogilvy Benson & Mather?"

"I would like you to try," he said.

"You've got me."

While driving me back to DDB, he said, "I don't believe we've talked about how much you'll be paid."

I told him that I was certain he would treat me fairly.

"I'll pay you twice what you're earning now," he said calmly.

When I could breathe again, I asked him if he knew how much I was earning now.

"No," he said, "but I'm certain you'll tell me."

A salary of $60,000 was unheard of in 1965, but given the speed and accuracy of the advertising business grapevine, it was heard of all over town in a matter of days. What made it such an occasion for gossip was not the starting figure alone, but the fact that I was just a Group Head, reporting to Clifford Field, the Creative Director.

Cliff was the sort of Englishman of whom it had been said that if he were any more English he would not be able to speak at all. He spoke in a barely audible mumble and called me "old boy" and "dear chap." It was Cliff who had been the author of all the best and most elegant work that the agency had turned out over the years; it was Cliff who had written the splendid British Travel series, including the gravely lyrical and stirring head-line: "Tread softly past the long, long sleep of kings." I felt honored to be working for him, and I told him so.

"Oh but you're not working for me, dear chap," he murmured. "Don't take my ridiculous title any more seriously than I do; we're both simply working for D.O."

I liked Clifford immediately and immensely.

To start, I was given a small group of people and two accounts, IBM Corporate and Sears Roebuck Corporate. It was only a couple of weeks after starting that I told David Ogilvy that he was paying me too much money for so little work.

He said that I had never asked him why he was paying me so much, but he would be glad to explain. He planned to reorganize shortly, he told me, in a quite new way. Cliff Field would no longer be Creative Director, and there would be no replacement for him. Instead, he intended to name five Creative Directors— he would call them Syndicate Heads—and I was to be one of them. Each of us would have a large group of accounts and people and would run our shows independently as if they were our own agencies. "Answering to me, of course," he added quite needlessly.

And then there was another matter. The agency was to go public shortly, and I would not have been employed long enough to get in on options prior to public issue. The large salary, he believed, would keep me from too much envy of the other Creative Directors, all of whom would make tidy sums.

"Of course you must have done well on DDB's public issue," he said, "so I can't feel too much sorrow for you."

I didn't tell him. What good would it have done?

We went public, and we reorganized.

David asked if I felt all right about it, if my salary was sufficient compensation for missing out on the big lump-sum handouts. Knowing it would do no good, I changed my mind and told him how I had missed out on DDB's public issue.

The next day I got a memo from him, reading as follows:

CONFIDENTIAL   March 3, 1966

DAVID HERZBRUN

Shelby tells me that if you stay here until you are 60, and never get an increase in salary, your nest egg in the profit sharing is likely to be about $292,000. That would buy you an annuity of $23,000 a year. You could afford to live in Portugal with a staff of at least six servants.

(signed) David

Greatly soothed by this information, despite never having had the least thought of retiring in Portugal, I put the memo in my file and out of my mind and turned my attention to the reorganization of the agency.

Jim Heekin was named President, the youngest in any major agency. I was nervous about working with him because I had known him slightly in our college years through dating roommates at Bennington, and I had come to an early conviction that he was a difficult and maybe slightly crazy person.

This conviction was not lessened when I read an interview with him in *Madison Avenue* magazine. The reporter asked him if there were anything he could think of that he would rather be than the youngest President of any top-ten agency, and Heekin said he would rather be Heavyweight Boxing Champion of the World. Then, to make it worse, he went on to say that he sometimes fantasized how it would feel to be standing in the center of the ring at Madison Square Garden with the second toughest man in the world out cold at his feet.

When David told a general meeting of the agency staff about the appointments of Heekin and we five Syndicate Heads, a young account man named Bill Phillips stood up to ask a question: "With all these changes, what's *your* title?"

The reply was loud, strong, and deliberate. "My title . . . is . . . David . . . Ogilvy."

I had lunch with Cliff to find out what had gone wrong. He said that I was not to worry, that he had, in fact, asked D.O. to remove him from the Creative Director's job. "The very best title in the agency business is Group Head,"he said. "You'll find that out now that you've stopped being one."

Cliff insisted that he be moved out of his big corner office and that I be moved into it. I objected, but he said that I would need the space for meetings and that the symbolism of the corner would be good for me in the upcoming struggle for position.

I hadn't forseen any struggle. After all, we each had our own accounts and people, so what occasion would there be for conflict?

Cliff looked startled. Then he switched back to the topic of the big office. "Trust me, dear fellow, you'll benefit by it. Agencies are like Orwell's *Animal Farm*, you know. 'All animals are

created equal, but some animals are more equal than others,'
remember?" He paused and was silent for a longish while. "I'm
afraid it's the pigs who always come out ahead," he said sadly.

Options granted before public issue went up for sale at a
ratio of 15 to 1, and Cliff came out handsomely with, I believe,
about $2 million. But, of course, nobody came out as well as
David.

A day or two after the issue, he practically bounced into my
office, his handsome face rosy with smiles. "This is a marvelous
business," he said. "It's a sort of money machine. You put in
white paper at one end, and it comes out green at the other." He
paused and settled back in one of my two enormous black
leather couches. "Have you any idea of how much money I'm
worth now?" he asked.

I told him I was sure it was a lot.

"Twenty-two million dollars!" he said. "What do you think
of that?"

"I think I have an interesting business proposition for you,"
I said.

"What do you have in mind?" he asked cautiously.

"Well, you give me a million dollars . . . ." I said.

"And?"

"That's all," I said. "You just give me a million dollars."

"Why should I do that?" he asked reasonably.

"Because if you did, you wouldn't notice the difference; your
standard of living would be the same if you only had twenty one
million. But if I had one million, I would move right up to your
class, and maybe I'd have a chance to do you a favor some day."

He laughed uproariously. And then, when the laughing
stopped, there was a moment, an instant, when I could see that
he was actually going to do it, going to make me a millionaire in
a stroke.

But the instant passed, and we both knew what had almost
happened. Months later he said that he had very nearly done it,
just for the wonderful story it would have made. "I'd have dined
out on that for years," David said.

I asked him what made him change his mind.

"If I were an American, I'd surely have done it. If I were an Englishman of a certain kind, I might have done it. But I am a Scot, so it was quite impossible."

I told him that it was the second time that an accident of birth had kept me from being rich.

My group at the newly renamed Ogilvy & Mather (Who was Benson? Who, for that matter, was Mather?) had all of David's pet personal accounts, the cornerstones of the agency. I had British Travel, Schweppes, Hathaway Shirts, Zippo Lighters, International Paper, and Sears Roebuck. I also had a new product assignment in the detergent category, a line extension product for Ban deodorant and Stripe toothpaste, all from Lever Brothers. These were my first experiences with packaged goods.

I won't write about packaged goods or Lever Brothers because I didn't have one amusing or interesting experience with them.

British Travel Association was the account I was most excited to get. I wanted to try my hand at writing as well as Cliff Field. I wanted, at least, to turn out some advertising that he would admire. What's more, the BTA business would give me a chance to travel extensively in Great Britain.

David asked me to see him for a briefing. "This is the new campaign," he said, passing me a layout. "The headline is meant to be the same in every ad, which will save you trouble. You'll only have to find the right pictures to fit your subjects."

The headline was "Visit Britain, Ancient and Mod."

I told him I thought the line was awful, that *Mod* was a particularly distasteful word representing a new and scary lifestyle that American tourists would not find very inviting.

David said that it was only a smart new way to say *modern* and that the BTA people were particularly insistent that the new "swinging England" phenomenon be included in the advertising.

I told him that *Mod* these days referred only to one of two warring groups of young thugs, the Mods and the Rockers.

"Of course there's some understanding of that," he said,

"but in this context everyone will understand that we're only using the title of the Church of England hymn book."

I told him that very few Americans would make that connection, but he was unconvinced so I moved on to attack the basic concept. I said that American tourists visited Britian only to see what was old because we didn't have any of that here. We were enchanted by visions of castles, ruins, ancient pubs and inns, thatched cottages, half-timbered villages, and the like. We had the Beatles here and had made a start at adopting the miniskirt. Nobody would spend money to see more of that when we were getting more of it here every day. But Westminster Abbey and the Houses of Parliament weren't coming to the United States for a visit.

(That was some time before London Bridge moved to Lake Havasu City.)

David said that the research they had done showed that Americans thought of Britain as old-fashioned, behind the times, conservative, and peopled by very cool, reserved citizens. The British Tourist Authority wanted to change all that. And besides, the campaign had been enthusiastically bought by them; it was too late to unsell it.

I looked at the layout again and held it up for David. "Do you really want to run this?" I asked. The ad showed two side-by-side photos, each long and narrow. The left-hand picture was of an old inn, half timbered and beflagged; and the other shot was of a new and rather ugly high-rise hotel—ancient and mod in contrast. The trouble was in the scale.

"You've got either a Brobdingnagian inn or a Lilliputian hotel, depending on how you look at it," I said.

David considered, then suggested that we bring the inn down in size to be proportionate to the hotel. I pointed out that an inch-high inn would lack something in charm. He suggested that I find a way to solve the problem. I would be allowed to change the layout, if I had to, but the headline was sacred.

I worked, without an art director, to figure out some situations that would combine ancient and modern in a single shot, and finally came up with a half dozen or so. One was a picture of a miniskirted bird walking arm in arm with a kilted Scott. Another was a pair of long-haired boys and a pair of bewigged barristers passing and staring at each other in Lincolns Inn Fields. A third, I recall, was a shot of—and through—a Henry Moore sculpture with an 11th century keep in the background.

The BTA people surprisingly agreed, but they insisted that the pictures be taken by their staff photographer, Barry Something. I had seen a lot of Barry's work and was not encouraged. He had spent two decades touring every corner of Great Britain to find picturesque or historic sites where he would camp out, for weeks if necessary, waiting for the skies to clear and the sun to shine. His pictures never included people, so they wouldn't go out of date as fashions changed. The good news was that they were all properly exposed and all in nice, sharp focus.

Since I was not allowed to hire a photographer who was used to working with models and who could shoot fast, I decided that I would have to get a camera and back up Barry's work myself. David agreed to have the agency buy a Nikon and a huge assortment of lenses for my use on the trip.

I am not now, nor have I ever been, a photographer. I went to see Onofrio Paccione, Art Director of the Year and one of the best of photographers, for a litte advice. Paccione—Patch to his friends—was a friend, and he agreed to give me some of his wisdom.

Patch, a small and dapper man who looked like a successful jockey, was precise in his movements as he showed me how to disassemble and reassemble the camera and how to change lenses.

"Okay," I said, "but how do I *use* the thing?"

"Read the instructions," Patch said.

"There's got to be more to it than that," I said.

Patch thought about it a while as we sipped our espresso and Averna, then he brightened up. "Sure," he said, "I almost forgot. You've got to know about film."

"What about it?" I whispered, poised to take technical notes.

"Film is the cheapest part of any shoot," Patch said. "Just swear to shoot at least four rolls of film for every picture you want. One of those 144 pictures has got to be good. That's all there is to it."

"There's got to be more than that," I said.

"Yeah." Patch said. "The other part is don't tell anybody that's all there is to it."

One other British Travel story:

My client, a man with the lovely name of Len Lickorish, wanted me to do an ad about the new GPO (General Post Office) Tower that dominated London. It is a graceless, ugly structure that features a revolving restaurant, which was a new idea at that time. I did my best to resist, but Len was insistent.

I delivered an ad that showed the GPO Tower, looming nastily over a row of handsome Georgian houses. The headline read, "We're still building bloody towers."

Len winced and then started reading the copy. It began, "The new General Post Office Tower Restaurant offers the best possible view of London because it is the only place in London from which one can't see the new General Post Office Tower."

Len looked up from the copy. "If I take your point properly," he said. "you'd really rather not do an ad on this subject."

Cliff Field prepared me for my first meeting with Commander Whitehead of Schweppes. "Teddy Whitehead's got a problem," he muttered to me. "He's getting on, you know, and he presents what a young audience might take as a rather, uh, geriatric image for Schweppes. He knows it, he's seen the research, so you'll have to do a lot of new campaigns for him."

"Why a lot?" I asked. "Why not one good one?"

"Because, of course, he won't buy any campaign that doesn't have him in it," Cliff said. Then he lowered his voice even more than usual, and I very nearly had to put my ear to his lips to hear his mumble. "The one thing you must know in order to deal with Teddy," Cliff confided, "is that his brain is the size of an aspirin tablet."

Whitehead was still a handsome man, tall, lean, and impressive, but his famous beard was shot with grey, and there was a web of fine wrinkles around his eyes. He reviewed several storyboards with little interest and no sign of displeasure or even comprehension. He agreed to think about them, and I had a notion that this would be a slow process.

I had also brought a new campaign of magazine ads that were to be shot in backgrounds of the American Revolution: Whitehead posed by an 18th century cannon; Whitehead galloping on horseback ("The British are coming again!"); Whitehead scanning the reader, presumably the horizon, from the forepeak of a naval sailing vessel. He liked them right away, of course, and we made arrangements to shoot in the Williamsburg, Yorktown, and Jamestown area as soon as possible.

Don Tortoriello was my art director. He hired Harry Hamburg, who was a still photographer then, to do the job. I was delighted because Harry was not only a fine photographer but a very funny man and pleasure to travel with.

Harry flew to Williamsburg, while Don and I drove, each in our own car, because I took Ellen with me. We wanted to stop in Washington for a day or two on the way to visit with family.

We arrived on time to meet Harry and then had to wait for several hours for Don to arrive. When he did, it was in his new toy—a white MG TF, the model with the ducktail rear end and flaring front fenders. Its grill and bumper were encrusted with British and continental racing badges.

He looked up at us and said proudly, "What do you think of the car?"

Harry, without hesitation, said, "I think it's a wop's conception of English history."

One unforeseen problem with Whitehead was that he didn't know how to smile. At least not with a camera pointed at him. He would go rigid and military. When Harry insisted on a smile, he would produce a ghastly rictus of death, his lips pulled back tightly against his teeth.

I told Harry about the aspirin-sized brain. "Maybe you'd better handle him the way you'd handle a child model," I suggested. "Kid around with him, get him to laugh naturally. You can do it; you're a funny man."

Harry said, "There's only one thing his class of Englishman thinks is funny, and that's bathroom humor."

He got Teddy arranged in the right pose with the cannon, got his camera ready, and called out to the commander, "Say *shit!*"

Teddy exploded with laughter.

"Pretty good," Harry said, "but you didn't say it, I did. Go on, say *shit!*"

Whitehead said it shyly and slyly, with a rather endearing naughty schoolboy smile.

"Louder!" Harry commanded.

"*Shit!*" roared Teddy, then laughed till tears came.

For the next three days—in the wood, on foot, and on horseback, on the deck of the man of war—Harry shot as Whitehead shat; and the word never failed to produce the desired results. He eventually got accustomed enough to it that the hilarity was replaced by a natural, warm smile, and we came home with the best pictures ever taken of him.

D.O. came in to my office one day and tossed a thick manila envelope onto my desk. "I think I've just made the biggest mail-order purchase in history," he said. "Open that envelope and see what I've bought."

What I saw was a collection of photographs of the exterior and interiors of a splendid French chateau and its gardens, plus aerial photos of it and its extensive fields, woods, and vineyards.

"Really mail order?" I asked. "You mean you've never seen it, and you've actually bought it?"

He had. He'd had to act quickly because it was going at a very low price and other potential buyers were beginning to show interest. I didn't know what a low price, or a high one, would be for such a place, but I said that I was sure it had cost a bundle.

"It's actually a bargain," David said. "It's an historic land-mark, so the French government gets to pay half the upkeep."

He then began to review the photos with me, explaining what each room was for, what changes he intended to make, how he wanted the gardens enlarged, and so on.

When we got to the aerial views, he indicated the vineyards. "I make a rather good little wine," he said.

I recently told that story to an Ogilvy Creative Director who said that it was in fact a very bad little wine.

He and a group of other O&M people had visited David at the chateau. When lunch was served and the wine poured, David told them, before proposing a toast, that the wine had come from "those vines you can see, right over there."

They all had a sip, and one of the guests said, "It doesn't travel very well, does it?"

Sears Roebuck was a pleasant corporate account for which the agency had produced a distinguished collection of warm, hu-man ads, mostly two-page spreads in magazines. They were in no way intended to sell merchandise but to create positive feel-ings about Sears.

When Sears advertised to sell things, they did it them-selves, almost exclusively in newspapers plus, of course, the cat-alog. They were the largest single advertiser in the United States and an enormously tempting target for the agency.

One day, the agency hit the target.

We convinced Sears that it was necessary for them to try television as a medium for selling goods. The statistics were in-arguable. Newspapers were going out of business everywhere, TV viewership was skyrocketing, and TV cost per thousand viewers was plummeting.

Sears bought the argument and told us to get started on creating a campaign for them. They were realistic enough to know that this was a kind of work that nobody in their vast advertising department was going to be able to do.

The job was enormously complex. We realized going in that we would need to create and produce a staggering number of spots because Sears was a complete department store and every department would want to be on the air with some consistency. To make it even more complex, practically no department could be served nationally with a single spot during its promotional week, due to regional and climate differences. Snow tires, for example, would be a major advertised item in the cold months, but only in the northern states. For the Tire-Batteries-Accessories Department in its sale period, something else would be needed in the southern tier.

The same held true of apparel and sporting goods, and even less obvious things such as tools and home furnishings had different peak selling seasons for varying kinds of merchandise depending on region.

To create the advertising that could do this required a quick beefing up of staff. I hired writers, art directors, TV producers, and finally a business coordinator for the syndicate just to keep track of who was doing what and which stage of the work each project was in.

We had a good presentation at Sears in Chicago. They approved the campaign and, two weeks later, approved production estimates on seventeen television commercials packaged with six different production companies in New York, Chicago, Los Angeles, and Miami.

More than half of my Sears group were in production while the rest were developing storyboards for the second round. We began to see how we would work and were no longer awed by the size and complexity of the job. The flow charts prepared daily by the coordinator looked good, and as a couple of the simpler spots moved into postproduction in New York, I was shown rough cuts that made me happy and calm.

Then, one nice sunny day, Jim Heekin called me from Chicago.

"Stop all Sears production immediately," he said.

"You're kidding?" I asked hopefully.

"I am not kidding," Jim said grimly. "I don't care if a spot is a day away from being finished or if it's in the middle of shooting. I want all of it brought to a screeching halt. Now. And don't ask me why. I'll see you tomorrow morning." He hung up.

There was nothing to do but follow my President's orders. I called in Jack Silverman, my broadcast production chief, and told him what to do.

"My God," he wailed. "I can't even reach some of these units; they're on location in Christ knows where."

I told him to do his best.

"Did you tell Heekin what kinds of penalties we're going to have to pay?" Jack asked. I told him that we hadn't talked about money. He rushed out to start phoning, and I sat quietly, feeling a little dazed. I couldn't imagine what could possibly have gone wrong.

What had gone wrong was Heekin.

The top client at Sears had said he sure hoped we were right in our decision to have no format to our advertising, but to do for each product whatever seemed right for it. He expressed a lingering doubt and a wistful longing for a recognizable Sears look, maybe with a slogan and even a theme song. He wanted some reassurance.

What he got was Heekin telling him he was absolutely right, that he had the same doubts himself, that we were fools to have sold him on what we were producing, and that he would stop everything, have the agency pay for all costs to date, and come back in two weeks with a new campaign.

"Didn't you try to convince him we were on the right track?" I asked.

"No, because I don't think we are."

"Why didn't you bring this up before we presented the work in the first place?" I asked.

He told me it was a waste of time to talk about the past and let's just march on; we had a major presentation to make in two weeks.

I got my troops back home, told them what had happened, and got them started. If we had to do a format and a theme song, so be it, but I wanted it done in a way nobody had ever seen before.

They paired off and began working. And at the same time, so did everyone else in the agency.

It was my first experience with a Gang Bang.

The idea of putting five creative groups in competition was something I had heard of, naturally, as one has heard of cannibalism or ritual murder among certain savages. At Doyle Dane Bernbach, it was a thing that was never done, and I hated it right away.

I asked Ogilvy to put a stop to it, but he demurred. He had often done such a thing, and even if it had not produced better advertising than letting one responsible group do its work, it had at least produced a huge pile of storyboards and alternatives to show the client. A lot of the work would be awful, he agreed, but the client would never notice the quality, only the impressive quantity.

I asked who would judge the work and select the winner.

David said that he preferred not to do that himself. We would all present to the agency's plans board, whose members would rate each campaign on a ten-point scale. If that didn't produce a clear winner, it would at least narrow the field. Then he, Jim Heekin, and Jock Elliott (O&M's Chairman) would make the final choice.

My group prepared to present one campaign, the single best idea we could come up with. During the first days, teams brought me ideas to sort out, reject, help refine. Then I settled on one campaign theme and asked the remaining teams to do specific commercials within the campaign.

I learned only a couple of days before the plans board presentation that the other Syndicate Heads, now called Creative Directors, were presenting anywhere from three to five campaigns. Some of my people pressed me to work up a couple of the ideas I had rejected, but I refused.

The conference room had been arranged like a small theater with the members of the plans board facing a podium. All around the room were stacks of storyboards, turned face to the wall. Since Sears was still officially my account, I was on first. I walked to the podium carrying my slim load of six storyboards, one for each of six products, all in one format.

The presentation went well. I could feel the approval of the board. When I was finished, there was a pleasant round of applause. I had started presenting at ten o'clock and was finished well before eleven.

The rest of the presentations took the rest of the day. It was nearly five o'clock when the Plans Board members handed their tally sheets to David Ogilvy, who analyzed them while everyone else milled around and nervously chatted and smoked.

He called the group to order, thanked everyone for his or her effort and for the high quality of the work, and then read out the point scores for each campaign, starting with the lowest score.

Mine won by a stunning margin.

Everyone congratulated me and my group as they left the conference room. I stayed behind with David, Jock Elliott, and Jim Heekin. When we four were alone, I said that I was pleased and relieved and already looking forward to our presentation to Sears.

"We're not presenting your campaign," Heekin said. "We're presenting Reva's, the one she recommended."

"But that didn't even come in second," I objected.

"That's not the point," Heekin said. "The three of us agree with the plans board that your campaign would probably sell more *for* Sears, but we also feel that Reva's campaign will be easiest to sell *to* Sears."

He and Jock got up and left. David put a sympathetic hand on my shoulder and asked me how I felt.

"Unaccustomed," I said. "It's the first time I've been in a whore house without having any fun."

David laughed loudly and trotted off down the hall to tell Jim and Jock the wonderfully witty thing I had said. I went home to tell Ellen that I thought I was at the end of my time with Ogilvy.

I came in early the next morning and went straight to David's office. He was expecting me; two coffee cups were waiting on the table in front of his couch. I sat down, and as he poured I said, "I guess I'd better go."

"Oh yes," he replied. "You'll certainly have to go."

He told me to take my time, two or three weeks, more if I needed it, to figure out what I would do next; and until I had made arrangements, he would withhold any announcement or mention that I was leaving. He asked if I had any ideas about where I would like to go.

I had thought of nothing else since the previous afternoon, and all I knew was that there was no agency I wanted to work for. I had never wanted to work for any agencies other than DDB and Ogilvy & Mather.

"Surely you could go back to Doyle Dane Bernbach," David suggested.

I could, of course; Bernbach loved to take people back, loved to say, "They always come back; they can't be happy anywhere else." But I didn't want to go back unless he asked me to. I didn't want to come back with my tail between my legs.

"I've been thinking of consulting to a few ad agencies," I said. "Maybe get a modest retainer from five agencies who might occasionally want the kind of work I do."

David looked interested. "Have you thought about what you'd charge and how many days you'd commit to each agency"

I had, but only in the most general way

"I suggest you think about it carefully for a few days. When you think you have a formula that works, let me go over it with you."

The first formula I came up with was easy enough. I figured that I could get a retainer of $12,000 a year from each of five agencies and make what I was presently making. I would charge at the rate of $250 a day, which would give each agency 48 days of my time per year, for a total of 240 working days.

David said it was completely wrong; that nobody would want to hire me unless I was outrageously expensive. I should charge $500 a day, giving each agency only 24 days a year. And I should sell my services to seven agencies. That way I would commit only 168 days a year and would take in $84,000. I would need the money, he told me.

When I expressed doubts about selling myself at $500 a day, David swept them away. "I'll be your first client," he said.

Before I could comment, he picked up the phone and called Shelby Page, our Comptroller. "Shelby," he said, "please make out a check for $12,000 to David Herzbrun and have your secretary bring it up right away."

I told him I'd much rather he pay me monthly, that I didn't need all that money in hand, but he insisted that I would need it. "You will have to rent an office. I want you in the city every day, not working at home in Connecticut. I want your office to be within ten minutes of mine, which will put you in the high-rent district. And I want you to hire a secretary. I detest dealing with answering services."

I was still worried about accepting a $12,000 check in advance. "What if I get a terrific job offer before I've worked it off?" I asked.

"If you'll promise not to take a job for three months, I promise to use the twenty-four days you owe me in that time," David said.

I said I'd get started right away. I finished my coffee, took the check from Shelby's secretary, and thanked David.

"As soon as you have a secretary, have her call my secretary and make an appointment. Meanwhile, I'll write a staff memo about all this."

I found an office right on 48th Street, diagonally across from Ogilvy & Mather. It was two rooms sublet from a fledgling dating service, the first such enterprise I had ever heard of. It was a one-man operation, and the man was hardly ever in the office. I couldn't imagine what he was out doing all the time. Test dating, maybe.

For a secretary, I hired a young woman named Margaret Joyner, whom I had known for a while as a regular on the 5:25 Bar Car. I took her word that she could type and bookkeep; all I really knew about her was that she was very smart, incredibly well-read, and possessed of a bitingly sardonic wit. I thought, wrongly as it turned out, that I could transform her into a copywriter, as I knew I wouldn't have work enough to keep a full-time secretary busy.

Once Margaret had convinced the telephone company that our need for phones was on the same level as a national emergency, she phoned David's secretary, a man named Harry, and got me put through to D.O. He set up a date for the next morning, telling me to be prepared to spend two hours with him and take a lot of notes.

After asking me where my office was and being delighted with the address, he said that he was going to spend a couple of hours making phone calls. All I was to do was sit at his desk and make notes about the calls. I was mystified, but only until the first call. David spoke with the President of a major agency, telling him about me and telling him why he should retain me as a creative consultant. He was at his most persuasive, which is more persuasive than most people ever get to see. He laughed, argued, charmed, and all but gave orders that I was to be retained immediately, sight unseen.

David repeated this performance perhaps ten times, in each call taking the time to make a little small talk first, tell a little joke, create a warm mood before going into his pitch.

I took notes about each call. The entire process lasted nearly two hours. When it was done, David said, "I'll give you two weeks to follow up on those calls before I put you to work. Let me know how you do."

I did just fine. I had my six other retainers before the two weeks were gone. I called David and said I was ready to work off my debt.

◆ ◆ ◆

David did as he said he would, used all twenty-four days of my time in less than three months and then never called me again.

My other clients, when they recovered from Ogilvy's charm, seemed a bit dazed, wondering why they had retained me and how they could use me. They made vague attempts to fit me into projects during those first three months or so and then just gave it up. Their checks kept coming in every month, and Margaret had no work to do but post the amounts in a ledger where she also kept a record of our few expenses.

I realized that none of my seven agencies would renew their contracts, and I made no effort to pitch others because it was clear that this was no way to make a living, only a straight path to limbo.

I filled some of my time doing free-lance jobs. I went to museums. I walked around the city a lot. I had long lunches with friends. And between times, I worried a lot about when to look for a job and where to look for it. It was a year of treading water.

This dim and feckless period ended when Bob Levenson called to say that he and Bill Bernbach wanted me to come back, to run the American Airlines creative group.

I rode on the train every day with Jack Dillon, who had been doing American Airlines and had been trying with no success to get off the business for quite a while. The client liked him a lot, Bernbach was happy with the work, and they resisted Jack's pleas.

I asked him how he had finally talked his way out.

"I told Bernbach I had been on the account longer than World War II," Jack said.

He explained the complexity of the business. The agency had to create over 300 new newspaper ads every year, because each destination had different things to promote. We also had a national image campaign that was made up of about a dozen magazine ads and seven or eight TV spots. And as a little side effort, we had to write nearly 1,000 radio scripts a year, just for "Music Till Dawn." But those were no problem; they were all written by one man, George Rike, who wrote newspaper ads in his spare time.

Jack said it wasn't a bad account, but that any account began to feel bad after you'd been on it for four years. He advised me to take the job.

I walked with him to DDB's office on West 43rd Street and rode up in that familiar elevator to that familiar floor to tell Bob Levenson that I was happy to be coming home to start my fourth life at DDB.

THE ART OF THE POSSIBLE

I had been away for more than two years, and shortly after my return I began to feel that coming back had been a mistake. Something hardly definable but very noticeable had changed. The work was still very good, sometimes brilliant, but the common enthusiasm had vanished. People were working behind closed doors, and nobody was saying, "Have you seen that great campaign that Whozis and Whatzis are working on?"

Bernbach seemed glad to have me back, but our relationship was still not terrific, and he took every opportunity to be sharp and negative with me. I had expected that Bob Gage, who had been working with Dillon on American, would be a good buffer between Bill and me, but he chose to get off the account too and to work with Jack on Polaroid.

I was given a new art director, Marvin Fireman, who Bernbach took an instant and strong dislike to. This took some of the pressure off me, but still made for uncomfortable meetings whenever Bernbach was present.

Marvin was a very intelligent, intensely neurotic, and voluble man. He liked to call me late at night, waking Ellen and me, to talk at length about his worries about the work we were doing and his fears that Bernbach hated him and was going to fire us both.

There was nothing wrong with the work we were doing, but nothing very right about it either. We were getting a lot of pressure from the client, and the agency wasn't pressing back in the old way. American decided that what was wanted was a slogan and a theme song because United, with its "Fly the Friendly Skies" song was becoming a major threat. Knowing the agency's long-standing aversion to both slogans and jingles, Marvin and I went to see Bernbach.

"Why are you guys always so argumentative?" he asked sharply. "If they want a slogan and a jingle, just do it. But do it well. We have no rules here that say jingles and slogans are wrong. I once made a real brand out of Cresta Blanca wines with a ten-second radio jingle." He sang the familiar little tune, "*C-R-E-S-T-A . . . B-L-A-N-C-A. Cresta. Blanca.*"

I wrote "Fly the American Way," a jingoistic bit of trash that was loved by all concerned and was set to music by Mitch Leigh, who was King of the Jingles before going on to write *Man of LaMancha.*

Mitch was Bill Bernbach's favorite composer and did all of the music for DDB commercials. I believe he was under some sort of contract with the agency, but whatever the arrangments, creative teams had no say in who would do the score for their commercials. It was always Mitch Leigh. As a result, Mitch never listened to anything the creative teams had to say. Actually, I had nothing to say, but had a lot of questions that went unanswered. I had never been involved with a jingle before and had never been to a music recording session.

I remained uninvolved with the jingle but was allowed to go to the recording session, which was deafening and mystifying. Working with Mitch was like being run over by a truck, except that it called you "Baby."

Marvin Fireman vanished. Frank Camardella was my new art director. I took on a bright new copywriter as my Assistant Group Head, a witty and tough-talking kid named Marvin Honig. He took much of the load off me, leaving me free to do a few commercials with Frank. Nothing much really happened that fall and winter, and especially nothing happened to make me feel that it had been a good idea to try to come home again.

With the arrival of spring, everything happened, all at once.

It was politics, and the agency was right in the middle of it.

Eugene McCarthy's antiwar movement was gathering steam. A large group of DDB people, spearheaded by David Reider, was contributing time and talent to create McCarthy's advertising.

There was jubilation when Lyndon Johnson, seeing the

strength of the Viet Nam protest, announced that he would not run for another term. The high mood was considerably dampened when Hubert Humphrey declared his candidacy and when, a few days later, the agency announced that DDB would do Humphrey's campaign.

A questionnaire went out to the Copy Supervisors to determine who would be willing to work on the Humphrey account. It seemed that everyone in the agency was either a McCarthy supporter or a Republican, except me. I was a kind of old-fashioned Populist Democrat and, until his support of the Viet Nam War, I had always admired Humphrey. So I had answered the questionnaire yes.

On May 14, Bernbach phoned me and said, "You're off American. You're on Humphrey." I immediately started a journal, and those were the first words I wrote in it.

Ken Duskin was assigned to be my partner. I found it an unexpected choice. Ken was a superb art director whose taste for elegance found its best expression in fashion ads. It had never occurred to me that he had any interest whatever in politics. I guess I just couldn't take seriously a man who dressed in a black velvet suit with a violet necktie and a matching silk handkerchief in his breast pocket. The months that followed changed my mind, if not Ken's style.

The next morning, Ken Duskin and I went to Bernbach's office, where I wrote the next entry in the journal. Bill said, "We three will change history. Our job is to let the young know what this man is and has been, long before fashion caught up with him."

Fashion? Caught up with him?

He told us we were to fly to Washington in two days to board the Vice President's jet and fly with him to Maine. Some time during the flight we would have a chance to meet with the man.

At the end of the day I went for a drink with my friend Dave Larson to get some advice about working on a presidential campaign. Dave had been part of the Lyndon Johnson campaign team in 1964.

He had one piece of advice, which he urged on me strongly. "Don't try to convince anyone personally. Just make ads. When people talk politics, don't talk; just listen. If you don't do this, you will turn into a make-believe maven, and you will lose all your friends."

The next day all my friends began to phone.

Frank Jacoby, a documentary film maker, called to say that he had spoken highly of me last night to Norman Sherman, Humphrey's press secretary. He also asked me to put in a good word for him if there was a chance to suggest a documentary man for the campaign.

Selven Feinschreiber called to warn me obscurely about someone named Julius Kahn.

Don Woolf called to say that Senator William Benton (founder of Benton & Bowles) had pressed Humphrey to use Walter O'Meara as an advertising consultant and that Humphrey had written to O'Meara who, following the DDB appointment, had gracefully refused. Don wondered if DDB might like to retain O'Meara who, not incidentally, was Don's father-in-law.

There were a lot of calls like those, but the one call that gave me something to think about came from Fred Papert and Monte Ghertler, who asked me to forget Humphrey and join Papert Koenig Lois to take on Bobby Kennedy's campaign instead. It was a killer offer, including a lot more money than I was making and assurance of an Associate Creative Director's job when the campaign was over.

I told them that I was booked for a meeting the next day with the Vice President, that my reactions to him would determine what I would do, and that I would let them know the day after. They agreed to wait.

There was something about Bobby Kennedy I didn't quite like, but there was no question that he was saying all the things I thought should be said. And then there was the Kennedy glamor, the charmed circle that I could, with a simple *yes*, step into, while stepping out of the growing discomfort of Doyle Dane Bernbach.

I began to hope that I would hate Hubert Humphrey when I met with him the next day.

Bernbach, Ken, and I, together with Arie Kopelman, who was to be Account Supervisor, and Lee Tredenari, our TV producer, flew to Washington. At the Military Air Command base, we boarded, not Air Force Two, but Humphrey's chartered TWA plane. This was politics, not government.

Bernbach sat up front with Humphrey and assorted dignitaries, and we sat in the back with newsmen and twin sister stews dressed in green and blue Humphrey dresses, with stripes designed to make an *H* on both front and back.

The twins smiled a lot, handed out plenty of food and drink, and kept a party atmosphere as we flew to Bangor. There we boarded a bus marked *Distinguished Guests* and drove to the University of Maine, following the limo that carried Humphrey and his aides.

Our first look at Hubert Humphrey took us by surprise. All of us had thought that he would be about middle height and definitely pudgy. We were not prepared for this athletically built man who was at least six feet tall and who radiated vitality.

And then he began to speak, and the room turned on.

Afterwards, Bill Bernbach said, "Just capture that quality, boys."

We boarded a little Fairchild twin-engine prop plane with the newsmen and flew to Augusta, where Humphrey was going to woo some key delegates at the Maine Democratic Convention.

We spent a few hours in a bus outside a Holiday Inn while Humphrey had a series of meetings. Finally we went to the convention and found it to be a miniature of the national ones we'd all seen on TV. Banners, balloons, straw hats, posters on sticks, pretty girls in white skirts and red blazers waving pom-poms and leading cheers—Maine had it all.

Maine also had Senator Muskie, who did the real politician's stunt of recognizing, one by one, almost every delegate and shouting greetings from the podium. "Hi, Bert! How's Sally? Margie! Say hello to Sam for me! Walter, I thought you were going to retire this year!" Muskie continued recognizing individuals without apparent error, but he somehow lacked the spirit for it, like a circus seal playing "My Country 'Tis of Thee" on squeeze-bulb horns. He seemed to be a grave and perhaps humorless man who was working gravely at being chummy and cheery.

He followed his mandatory memory performance with a speech, long and flat and tedious, then introduced Humphrey to an audience that at 9:30 P.M. was more than a little eager to get out of there.

Humphrey turned that audience on as if it were his first business in the morning. He greeted them like a clear, new day. They loved him, and they loved what he had to say. I made one note: "Men who fought in an integrated bunker in Khe Sanh cannot come back to a segregated slum."

By 10:30 we were back in the bus watching a large (for Maine) crowd of kids in their late teens and early twenties. They had McCarthy banners, antiwar banners, and, mysteriously, huge blue balloons. We saw them backlit by headlights, diffused by rain on the bus windows, excited and exciting.

"I wouldn't miss this for a girl," Ken Duskin said.

We flew back to Bangor where we boarded the 747 with a feeling of homecoming. The twins, Jan and Jerry, welcomed us all by name as we stepped in from the cold rain. They brought us drinks and shrimp cocktails. It was eleven at night, but we were too hyped up to feel tired, eager to see if we'd get to meet the Vice President on our return fight.

Norman Sherman, Humphrey's press secretary, came to tell us that he didn't think we'd get our visit tonight; Humphrey was tired and was not at all pleased with his speeches. What's more, we were running an hour behind schedule, and the V.P. would probably want to nap.

He was interrupted by another aide who told us that Humphrey wanted to talk to us right away. I grabbed my tape recorder, but the aide cautioned me not to take it, "The boss doesn't like that. He wants to talk freely."

In the front cabin, Humphrey sat facing aft, behind a large mahogany desk that was inlaid with a brass placque reading, "Hubert H. Humphrey, Vice President of the United States of America." On the bulkhead behind him was the vice presidential seal. Bill Bernbach introduced us, and Humphrey was careful to say our names correctly as he shook hands. He looked alert, eager, and well rested, showing no signs of weariness, impatience, or strain. I opened my notebook as he began to talk, and he stopped. "Don't you have a tape recorder with you?" he asked. I hurried off to get it.

These were only the first of hundreds of misdirections I was to hear in the coming months from people who knew exactly what Humphrey wanted, what he didn't want, what he could and could not do, what he thought, how he felt, what his mood was that day, what we should and should not present, and what was the right way to film him so he wouldn't look dumpy.

If politics is, as Bismarck suggested, the art of the possible, dealing with politicians may be the craft of the improbable.

We had a long, good talk with Humphrey. When it was done, I knew there was no way I could drop him and go to work for Bobby Kennedy.

We checked into the Madison Hotel at 3 A.M., agreed to meet for breakfast at 7, and tottered off to bed.

The next day I called Fred Papert and told him that I was going to stay with Humphrey. He wished me good luck and said that, when the election was over, he'd still like to have me at PKL. I told him the odds were good that I'd take him up on it.

That first day on the job was not to be the only twenty-two hour day we would put in during the next five months. It is, however, the only one I intend to describe in detail. To give the complete story of a political campaign so that the reader can understand the people involved, the issues, the shifting positions, the internal power struggles, the back scratching and back stabbing is to write a book. Maybe I'll write it some day, if anyone is interested in publishing such a history. For now, I'll keep to the advertising side of the story. And to my own experiences.

Ken and I started work, looking for a theme for Humphrey. We also had immediate needs, such as an ad announcing the openings of Humphrey campaign headquarters in a variety of cities. Those sounded like easy jobs, but we soon learned that it isn't easy to get politicians to sign off on anything.

It took me seven submissions of headlines to finally get approval by New York Citizens for Humphrey of a bland ad, to be signed by a couple of hundred supporters, headlined, "We want Humphrey. And we want you." The copy for this, our first ad, began, "The New York Citizens for Humphrey Headquarters is open for business."

"Whoa!" said our client, Lloyd Wright. "You have to learn how phrases can be misused out of context. Can't you just hear Bobby saying, 'Open for business? Of course. So are we. But we're also open for labor. And farmers. And the unemployed, and so on.'"

I tried, "If you believe in Hubert Humphrey, join the club." Of course I should have forseen that *club* is a rotten word in politics.

Next to be killed was "If you think Hubert Humphrey has a chance, you can improve the odds." Uh-uh. *Odds* made it sound like HHH had only an outside chance.

And so it went.

I forget what the final copy was like and what its first sentence was, but it couldn't have been very terrific because I didn't make note of it in my journal. What I did note was "learn to write defensively." What a lousy idea that is.

We worked for three weeks, second-thinking everything from the point of view of the Kennedy camp. Then, on the fourth of June, Bobby Kennedy was shot.

We, along with the entire nation, went into shock and mourning. The Humphrey team called Nixon's people and George Wallace's as well as McCarthy's and got a general agreement on suspending all political advertising for an undefined period of time.

Ken and I also got agreement from Lloyd Wright to cancel a trip we had scheduled for the next day to visit Humphrey at his home in Minnesota. Wright didn't want to cancel at first, but we pointed out that it could be made to look pretty bad if it got out that while Bobby Kennedy was dying, Humphrey was conferring with his ad agency.

On June 6, Kennedy died.

Ken and I decided that the agency should shut the next day while Bobby lay in state in St. Patrick's. Bill was in London, so we went to see Ned Doyle about the idea. He agreed, but said we'd have to clear it with Joe Daly, who was by then President of the agency. Ned went with us, and I put the proposition to Joe.

Joe thought for a moment, then said, "Okay, but just for half a day."

This seemed pretty grudging to me, and I said so. Joe said, "We close for half a day on Good Friday, and Jesus Christ died then."

I couldn't think of an answer for that, but Doyle could.

"But Joe," he said, "that was a long time ago."

During the next weeks we did a tremendous amount of work, but did no advertising that ran. We viewed dozens of hours of films of Humphrey talking to civic groups, talking to the National Press Club, talking to business leaders, talking, talking, talking. The stirring, inspirational quality that we felt when we heard him in person vanished on film. On film he seemed all bombast, bumble, and bullshit. He looked short and pudgy. He appeared weak, gutless. We tried to find positive moments when he was saying the right words in the right way, in hopes of cutting a spot. We looked and looked, late night after night.

The days were taken up with meetings, trips to Washington, planning sessions, a little creating of TV spots and newspaper ads, and those daily conferences with Bill Bernbach where we submitted our new work.

These conferences would leave us elated and flattered or depressed, humiliated, and angry—depending on Bill's mood. Lately his mood had been more often bad than good. Like us, he was beginning to lose faith in Humphrey. "He's got to deal with the Viet Nam issue," he said. "I'll say that to him the next time we meet. Meanwhile, why don't you boys write a couple of ads, maybe a commercial or two dealing with the issue. Maybe that will move him in the right direction."

We were nearly out the door when he called me back. "David, you should write a speech for him about the war thing. Make it a minute, maybe even two minutes. It's the kind of commercial we need."

I pointed out that I had no idea of what Humbert Humphrey's position was regarding Viet Nam, which would make it hard to write for him.

"I know," Bill said, "but if you write something all of us here would agree to, we can then find out if he'll agree to it too. If he won't, that will be a way of learning what he *does* think."

"Smoke him out," I said conspiratorially.

"Right," Bill said. "There's more than one way to skin a cat."

I left, with the image of smoked, skinned cat in my mind, and spent the rest of the day writing a Viet Nam speech commercial. It was good to get it out of my system, even though I knew that it would be rejected by everyone who stood between us and the Vice President. He would never get the chance to agree to it or not. He would never smell the smoke or glimpse the skinning knife.

On June 20, we flew to Washington to present our work, at last, to the Vice President and his staff and advisors. We had two huge portfolios full of ads and storyboards, some file film cut to commercial length, and some slides to project.

I was feeling depressed and apprehensive, a mood shared by Ken, Lee, and Bruce Alpert, our Account Exec. All three of us felt that our loyalty to Humphrey was ebbing fast, due to his refusal to speak out on Viet Nam or any other matter of importance. Since the campaign began, he had publicly spoken of nothing but the past, often the distant past. At the same time, our loyalty to Bill Bernbach was at an all-time low. His sharp temper and stubborn arrogance had wounded us all. We were looking forward to a long, and probably disastrous, day.

Arie Kopelman was already with Lloyd Wright when we

arrived to preview the presentation. Both of them were subdued and nervous, and I asked what the problem was. Wright explained that Humphrey was due to speak at a luncheon at the National Press Club in his first speech since Bobby Kennedy's assassination. Wright and Arie feared that the speech, which was to be on domestic issues, would be viewed by the press as an avoidance of the real and pressing issue and that they would rip Humphrey apart in the question period. They weren't concerned that this would do him any actual harm, but that it would leave him in a lousy mood for our presentation at three o'clock.

We met Dennis Askey, who was assistant to Lloyd and advisor to the campaign on black issues. Dennis took us to the Executive Office Building, across the street from the White House, to check out the room and set up for our meeting. After some delay with a security guard, who had not been told to expect us, we were shown into a large conference room adjoining the vice president's office.

Ken, Lee, and I went in to look at the office, a room at once imposing and gracious, with windows overlooking the side entrance to the White House. Ken immediately suggested an ad reading, "Help this man across the street."

We hung around, making up a few more joke ads to cheer each other up, waiting for a projector to arrive. When it finally came, Lee hooked it up and promptly found that the bulb was burned out and the take-up reel was out of order. Dennis went back to United Democrats for Humphrey to get a working projector.

While we waited for him to return, Lee told us stories about filming Lyndon Johnson four years earlier. "He picked his nose a lot," Lee said, "and he kept on calling for a 'boy' to bring him orange juice, which turned out to be half bourbon.

"One time we were filming LBJ with Lady Bird and the girls sitting by him, and Linda fell alseep while Johnson was talking. Jim Graham was acting as floor manager, with headphones on, while I was in the tape truck outside. I shouted to Graham, 'For Christ sake tell that dumb (expletive deleted) to wake up! Her father's speaking!' It came through Jim's phones so loud it woke her up, and she whined, 'That man shouldn't talk that way,' but Johnson just said, very gently, 'Now Linda honey, the man's right. I'll start over, and you just stay awake till I'm finished.'"

A few more stories like that, and finally Dennis arrived with a working projector. We set up and went to lunch at Sans Souci, slowly building on the mood we had started the day with, worrying that even as we ate, the press would be crucifying Humphrey, while half hoping they would force him into anger and a positive statement about Viet Nam.

When we returned from lunch, Bernbach and Wright joined us, elated by the Press Club speech. They told us the press was very warm, Humphrey was inspiring as usual, the questions were not hostile, and the answers were met with applause; the whole thing was a love-in.

People began to assemble for the presentation. We had not been told to expect a large group and had figured on dealing with only Humphrey, Lloyd Wright, Norm Sherman, and Ted Van Dyke, who I think was campaign manager. What we got was Senator Fred Harris and Senator Walter (Fritz) Mondale, cochairman of the Humphrey campaign; Ambassador John Grenowski, who had resigned his Polish mission to work for Humphrey; Orville Freeman, ex-Secretary of Agriculture and ex-governor of Minnesota; Jeno Paulucci, who had sold his Chun King food business for $60 million, backed Humphrey, and probably wanted someting; Lee Vann, Jeno's aide; Norm Sherman; Larry Hayes, executive director of United Democrats for Humphrey; Bob Short, director of Citizens for Humphrey; Dick McGuire, treasurer of United Democrats for Humphrey; Jerry Bush, Humphrey's speechwriter; Bob Squier, documentary filmmaker; Lloyd Wright; Dennis Askey; Bill; Arie; Bruce; Ken; Lee; and me; plus (inexplicably) Dr. Edgar Berman, Humphrey's friend, confidant, raconteur, and personal physician. Add the Vice President, who was not yet there, and there would be 24 people in the room, an unworkable crowd to present to.

After waiting nearly an hour for Humphrey to show up, it was decided to start without him. Bernbach got up and began to speak, but was almost immediately cut off by the phone ringing.

"It's probably Lyndon," Freeman said.

"Put him on hold," Harris growled.

Bill started again, but go no more than a sentence out when

Humphrey arrived. Everybody stood up. Then everybody sat down. Bill started for the third time. He spoke with his usual calm, deliberate presentation manner, something I was trying to learn from him. Presenting always made me a little nervous. I was sitting next to him, prepared to hold up ads and storyboards as needed. I dropped my lighter on the floor, and when I bent to pick it up, I saw that Bill's knees were shaking. So he had stage fright too! The difference between us was that he had learned to keep his under the table.

He finished his remarks about strategy and began to show ads, about six or seven of them. One was headlined, "For twenty years, he's been ten years ahead of his time," and went on to show a long list of accomplishments. "My God, I'm impressive!" Humphrey crowed. "Mondale! Harris! Did you know I've done all that?"

The last of the ads was just a headline with some dummy type following. It read, "But what has he done for us lately?" Bernbach explained that there was no copy for this ad because nobody had been able to answer the question with any substance.

For an instant Humphrey looked offended, but then said, "Don't talk to anyone but me on that. Just see me, and I'll tell you. I'll tell you enough to fill two or three of those ad pages."

We went on to show storyboards and edited film clips. Humphrey was positive and enthusiastic. He made some perceptive comments, some smart suggestions. I was beginning to feel good about him again.

And then he blew it. "I'm sorry, but I've got to go," he said. "I have to go give ice cream to Martin Luther King's children; I sure hope we get some pictures of that."

The meeting went on with media plans and budgets, arguments about where the money would come from and how to use it, all the usual stuff. I let it drone on while I thought about the day before, when Humphrey had been booed in Resurrection City at the Poor People's Solidarity March. Did he think they'd like seeing him feed ice cream to the King kids? If he had to use the Kings' prestige, he should have himself pictured conferring with Mrs. King, asking for her advice and counsel.

Then I reminded myself that I wasn't a politician or a strategist, but a copywriter. Stick to my craft, I told myself sternly. But out of habit, I was already acting like a politician. The meeting broke up, but Senator Harris held us as the goodbyes started.

"Mr. Bernbaum," he said, "everybody in Washington knows some of your people are doing' advertisin' for Gene McCarthy for nothin'. It's kind of a joke that Humphrey has to pay for what McCarthy gets for free. Some folks make a dirty joke from it. I want you to stop that from goin' on."

Bill explained that he could not stop it and would not stop it, and that he had had this matter out with Ted Van Dyke before agreeing to have the agency take on Humphrey's campaign.

Harris stared him down. "What would you say at the Volkswagen agency if some of your people were moonlightin' for Renault?" he asked.

"I would stop it," Bill said. "But this is not a reasonable analogy. This is politics, not products."

"Right!" Harris snapped back, "and the presidency is sure more important than a lil' German car."

"That's just the point," Bernbach said impatiently. "The presidency *is* important; it's a matter of personal conviction, and I can't ask people to stop working for what they believe in any more than I can ask people to work for what they don't believe in. All the Humphrey team are volunteers. I did not ask them, or force them, to work for you."

Harris remained unconvinced and stubborn, and the argument went on for a while longer. Bill referred to "kids on my staff" who were working for McCarthy, and Harris pressed him to know who and how many. Bernbach said he didn't really know for sure. Harris then asked at what level these "kids" were, his tone making it clear that he already knew the answer.

Bill made a mistake then. "Oh, maybe one good copywriter and one good art director," he said.

Harris thanked him with a sneer. I felt that he would never again fully trust us, and this could become a serious problem. Now he picked up the argument again, expressing his fear that the Harris-Mondale committee could be made to look foolish in Washington.

"It could be made to look worse than that," Bill said, "if

word were to get out that your committee insisted the agency muzzle the free expression of its employees—or fire them if they would not be muzzled."

Harris backed off, not satisfied but satisfactorily boxed.

The meeting ended awkwardly, but all of us knew that we had not yet heard the end of the discontent with our McCarthy supporters.

My cousin, Phil Herzbrun, a professor at Georgetown, took me to a real Washington party. Everyone there was in politics including, I realized to my astonishment, me. They all accepted me as a pro, and all of them, being Humphrey supporters, expressed delight in meeting me.

It felt great. In my own circle, at home in Westport, or in the office, everyone was supporting McCarthy. I had been feeling like a pariah, and now all these smart Washington insiders were making me feel like a star.

Our hostess, Jaye Smith, had just quit her job at Housing and Urban Development to work for Humphrey. She was eager to help me and said that her brother Pete would be tremendously useful for me to know. She phoned Pete and told him to come over right away.

Pete arrived about midnight. His full name was Senator Harrison Williams. He took me aside and whispered conspiratorially, "There are a lot of things I want to tell you about Hubert and his staff and the politics of this campaign, but for the moment my lips are sealed."

"Why?" I asked.

"Because I'm drunk," he said solemnly and sloped off into the crowd.

I saw him a couple of more time that night, but we never spoke again.

Fred Harris's distrust of Doyle Dane Bernbach showed up in late June in the person of Ross Cummings, an Oklahoma ad man who had done Harris's senatorial campaign.

He explained that Harris had asked him to work with us to "coordinate the promotional materials" and to "check out" our advertising. Cummings was a pleasant, rather deferential man who seemed embarrassed and uncomfortable doing what he had been asked to do. At the same time, he made it quite clear that he was going to do it.

He started by asking us to create a series of four brochures for mailings and for handouts at rallies. We agreed to do them, though we all felt it was a make-work request, a way for Ross Cummings to start to insert himself into the process.

Bernbach was a lot more concerned about Cummings than I was. I told him I thought Ross was a good guy who was just doing what his boss asked him to do. I didn't think he would cause us much trouble. Bill looked unconvinced.

As usual, his instincts would turn out to be better than mine.

We had been working for two months, Ken and I and our entire staff of copywriters and art directors that Bernbach often referred to when in Washington. The staff consisted of Bob Mackall and Ed Griles.

The four of us had worked impossibly long hours: endless days, weekends, and early mornings at hotel breakfasts. We had commuted steadily to Washington and occasionally to Minnesota. We had submitted more than thirty ads and TV storyboards and had thus far produced only one ad. It was for the New York branch of Citizens for Humphrey, a sort of tactical wing of our client, United Democrats for Humphrey.

We were all pretty strung out, but we didn't need more help; what we needed was a client who would and could act decisively and actually run some advertising.

Bernbach decided we needed more help. He asked Paula Green to work with us. I didn't welcome the action, not because Paula wasn't a first-rate copywriter (she was) but because she wouldn't react well to taking direction and criticism from me (she didn't). However, since there was no way that she could learn instantly the background we had learned during two months, she had to follow my lead. She was not gracious about it. I was not overly conciliatory. When we differed, as we did from the first, on matters of style and not just substance, the sparks flew. At the end of a day of battling with Paula about how one of her headlines should be punctuated, I took a break and went out for a cocktail, hoping to find relaxation at a favorite saloon. What I found was hardly relaxing.

Eddie Ferro, co-owner of the place, introduced me to a copywriter named Jerry Gross who worked at Lennon & Newell. Gross said that he had just been assigned to the Humphrey account. He claimed that L&N had just picked up Citizens for Humphrey, leaving us the UDH in Washington, a more or less advisory group that wasn't inclined to run any ads.

Gross was confused that one of our ads (the only ad) that had run the day before had been signed by Citizens for Humphrey.

I was equally confused by his assurance that Lennon & Newell actually had the account. He told me that they already had a man full-time in Washington who would be working with Short and Bob Pickett.

I hurried back to the agency to find Lloyd Wright in Arie Kopelman's office. Lloyd knew nothing about L&N and was clearly disturbed by it. He said that he thought it would have come from Harris and Cummings and that he would put a stop to it.

His tone carried very little conviction.

Colonel Arthur Elkins Hoffman, USAF, Ret., came to see Lloyd Wright and us on an introduction, he said, from newsman Martin Agronsky. He told us he wanted to show us a "fantastic fund-raising idea."

The colonel was a lean, fanatical-looking man who, with no prologue, opened his attache case and produced a stack of what looked like misshapen flapjacks colored in garish pink or bilious green. He passed one to each of us. The things were made of spongy plastic, spirally die-cut, and when pressed upward from the center proved to be very ugly hats. The colonel explained that they could be imprinted with Humphrey material on one side and with any local candidate's material on the other. The great idea, you see, was that they could be worn either side up. That meant we could get local candidates' organizations to buy them from us, and they wouldn't cost our organization a cent.

The price was ten cents each, if ordered in quantities of one million.

Lloyd was horrified. He tried, with no success, to cut off the colonel's sales pitch. The colonel, feisty and verbose, talked right through him. When he was done at last, Lloyd told him as calmly as possible that we weren't interested.

The colonel jumped to his feet and screamed at Lloyd, "You are a blithering idiot! It's no wonder that Humphrey's campaign is such a dud! You fools are going to lose this election for a fine man, and I'm going to tell Martin Agronsky who's to blame!"

He grabbed the spiral hats from us, slammed them back into his case, and shouted to us all, "I've made five million dollars in the last five years! Now tell me how much you've made! Jerks! Sheee-it!"

The colonel stamped out of the office and promptly stamped back in to collect his hat, not a spiral but a rakish Panama. He paused dramatically at the door before making his final exit.

"Goodbye, Mr. Wright," he said. "Goodbye gentlemen. And goodbye Mr. Humphrey! Sheee- it!"

Bernbach, Ken, Lee, Arie, Bruce, and I met at the airport on a stifling Sunday morning to visit with Humphrey at his home in Waverly, a suburb of Minneapolis. Much to our surprise, we were joined by Ross Cummings. Bernbach gave him a curt hello, then turned to Arie to whisper loudly, "Who asked him along? And why wasn't I told?" Neither Arie nor anyone else had any answers.

Lloyd Wright met us in Minneapolis and told us that we were not going to Waverly after all, but would meet in the staff suite at the Hotel Leamington.

Pickets were outside the hotel, but not the usual McCarthy supporters or war protesters. This group carried signs reading,

"George Burns for Secretary of State?" and "Does George Burns make foreign policy for Humphrey?"

None of us could explain the signs. I asked one of the demonstrators what they meant and was answered with a screamed torrent of abuse. A policeman led the demonstrator to a lock-up wagon. He went with no resistance.

Upstairs in the staff suite, we asked Norm Sherman what the George Burns people had in mind. He said, "This is the end of July. It's the official start of the crazy season. It happens on schedule every presidential year."

Colonel Hoffman had jumped the gun by only a few days.

We waited about an hour for the Vice President to arrive, and after greetings and handshakes, Bill started the meeting. He was very forceful about our feeling that Humphrey must talk about the future, not the record, and that he must be very specific. If we did talk about the past, as we wanted to do in "But what has he done for us lately?" it must be the very recent past, and it must be very specific.

Bill reminded him of this ad and that at our June 20 meeting Humphrey had told us to ask only him for facts to help us write it.

"Would you like them now?" he asked. "Have you got the time to hear them all?" He laughed happily. Then he turned to me. "Got your tape recorder and plenty of spare tape, David? Okay, let's go."

True to his word, Humphrey talked for quite a while. He was also very specific, giving us plenty of hard facts, dates, numbers, and impressive accomplishments. It was great stuff except that, embarrassingly enough, it was all about what he had done as mayor of Minneapolis, more than twenty years earlier.

We knew we'd never finish that ad.

Bernbach changed the subject abruptly and wonderfully to the Viet Nam problem.

Humphrey said, "The greatest tragedy of Viet Nam is the view that nothing else matters. We must break out of this and put the war in its proper perspective."

Bill asked what that perspective was, and Humphrey went into automatic, delivering a ten minute speech that we had heard a few times before.

When he was done, I asked him, "What are the 'lessons that we have learned from Viet Nam' that you have so often referred to? If you could tell us—lesson one, lesson two, lesson three, four, five— we'd have a great ad and a great commercial."

Humphrey laughed and said, "I knew somebody would ask me that some day." Then he said to Van Dyke, "Better get the policy boys to work up a paper on that."

Lee Tredenari told me that he had spoken to Bill a few days before about the lack of momentum we all felt in the campaign. It was August and the convention was a few weeks off, and nothing was planned to fill the gap except a couple of newspaper ads.

Lee had said, "It seems to me, Bill, that Humphrey just isn't catching fire. The public is cold towards him, and we've got to do something to get people interested. For instance, if he would debate McCarthy now, instead of waiting till the eve of the convention, people would tune in. It would be a safer time for him to do it, too. After all, he might not do well against McCarthy, and if that happens on the brink of the convention, he won't get a second chance. Maybe he ought to have two debates before the election; and even if they don't go wonderfully, we could sure pick out the good moments and cut a spot or two."

Lee said that Bernbach responded in a lukewarm way to the idea, not really catching fire either.

The next day, Bill asked Lee to show the tapes we had cut to his friend Peter Strauss, who owned WMCA. After Strauss had viewed them and had given his opinion, Bill said to him, "You know, Peter, I've been worried about this campaign. Humphrey just doesn't seem to be catching fire with the public. Last night I couldn't sleep; I lay awake for two hours or more thinking about what should be done, and I came to the conclusion that Humphrey shouldn't put off the debate with McCarthy until the eve of the convention. I think if they were to have two debates before the convention . . . ." and on to the end of Lee's proposal.

When he was done speaking, Strauss said fervently, "That's brilliant, Bill! That's just brilliant!" Lee said he thought it was a great idea too.

Bernbach grabbed the phone and called Arie. "Get me fifteen minutes with the Vice President as soon as you can next week!" he commanded.

If you want to read about the Democratic Convention of 1968, get a copy of Norman Mailer's *Miami and the Siege of Chicago*.

It's a great temptation to tell the story all over again—the hippies, the Yippies, the cops charging into the parks to evict the kids, all the while yelling, "Kill! Kill!" and whacking kids with their nightsticks—but this isn't the place.

I'll leave it alone and stay with the advertising part of the story, but not without saying that we went to Chicago with our spirits at low ebb, and all through that terrible week we felt worse every day. We felt worse about Hubert H. Humphrey, who got up from watching the TV and left the room every time the cameras cut from the happenings on the convention floor to the demonstrations and brutality in the streets, and who kept the blinds closed in the rooms overlooking Grant Park so that he wouldn't have to see the protesting crowd, the squads of police, the riot trucks.

We felt worse about Bill Bernbach, who suddenly seemed to lose his backbone and his iron will, who stopped defending any work we presented, and who was docile in taking orders from the political pros but fierce in giving those orders to us.

We felt worse about the political process and the people who ran that process. And finally, we felt worse about the condition of our country and the knowledge that what we personally were doing would do nothing to correct the condition and might, in fact, exacerbate it.

The troubles started with our first meeting in Chicago, where Senators Harris and Mondale were scheduled to introduce us to Larry O'Brien, and we were scheduled to show him our work.

We waited for them in a suite in the Hilton Tower. An hour passed as we tried with little success to make conversation. We had already been too much together and had little to say. There were Bernbach; Ken; Lee; Paula; Norm Tannen, who had recently come aboard as her art director; Mackall; Griles; Arie; Bruce; and me from the agency. Lloyd Wright and Dennis Askey were there for UDH.

Finally three men came in, not the three we had waited for, and introduced themselves as O'Brien's aides. Joe Napolitan was the leader, and with him were Ira Kappenstein and Julie Cahn, who must have been the Julius Kahn I had been warned so long ago to look out for.

Napolitan was a professional campaign manager and his boss, Larry O'Brien, was considered to be the infallible best in that profession. He had managed the Kennedys and had never lost an election. He was recognized as America's premier Kingmaker.

"Okay, Mr. Bernbach, let's see the stuff," Napolitan said.

"I'd rather wait for Mr. O'Brien," Bill said.

"O'Brien won't look at anything until I've gone through it first and screened out the garbage," Napolitan said. "So let's get started."

"We didn't bring any garbage," Bill said stiffly.

"That'll be a first," Napolitan said. "Now let's just see the stuff."

Bill began with a storyboard we all loved. It showed a circus elephant marching slowly backward into the distance to the sound of a circus march played at a very slow, draggy tempo. The voice-over said something about the Republican party on the march, backwards into the past.

The voice went on to give chapter and verse of some of the Republican party's plans to undo the social programs put in place in the last decade.

Bill was hesitant and nervous in his presentation. He read the copy in a low, shakey voice, almost a whisper, while Napolitan leaned forward and listened intently and without a flicker of expression.

When Bill was done, Napolitan promptly said, "Terrible."

Shocked, Bill asked him why.

"It's full of facts and figures; it's built on logic. People can't handle that. People can't absorb facts and figures and don't know how to follow logic. People deal with emotion; they vote emotionally. That commercial is as cold and unemotional as an arithmetic lesson."

"But," Bill began.

"What's more," Napolitan interrupted, "it is not a good visual spot; it doesn't use the full visual potential of TV."

Bill looked paler than usual, and we could see that he was outraged, but he remained oddly docile. He only muttered that we had a great record in TV and knew how to use it perhaps better than any other agency, but he did not defend the specific Elephant spot. He moved on to the next three spots, all of which were received with no comment from Napolitan or his boys. The fourth commercial, which showed a three-dimensional caricature of Nixon as a weathervane with his arms outstretched and pointing in opposite directions, did get a small murmur of approval. Napolitan liked the idea, but not the copy.

"Same as the Elephant spot. Too many facts. But it may be worth working on some more."

Bill presented fifteen storyboards that morning. All were judged to be garbage except "Weathervane." It alone survived to be shown to O'Brien and to many others, to be rewritten countless times. And it alone made it into production and was finally aired, though none of Humphrey's staff was ever particularly enthusiastic about it.

"Weathervane" is now considered a classic. It is certainly the most imitated political spot of all times and may even be the most imitated commercial of any kind.

I've been trying to avoid "and then I wrote" stories, but I couldn't resist taking pleasure in "Weathervane" while describing this otherwise sad and bitter campaign in which there was so little pleasure to be taken.

Rumors began growing that Ted Kennedy was available for a draft. At dinner, we all speculated on the possibility. It was exciting to think about, a breath of fresh air in an atmosphere growing increasingly fusty with cigar smoke, ever more fakey with all those bands and straw hats and all that solid, fat-bellied, broad-shouldered arrogance of the pro polls.

"Kennedy hasn't a chance," Bernbach said, "but I wouldn't mind too much if it did happen, because I'm sure we could get the account. Besides," he added hurriedly, "it might be the best thing for the country. He could give us a young image and a new sense of excitement, unite us."

Later in the evening, Bill began to hope that Teddy could actually make it. "If those Kennedy boys saw those commercials of ours," he said, "they'd buy them all right on the spot. They have guts. Our stuff is just too strong for O'Brien's boys and the Humphrey staff."

Later still, in the car that drove us back to the hotel, he said, "You know, most of our work will still stand up if Ted gets the nomination. It's all anti-Republican and anti-Nixon. None of it's pro-Hubert. We haven't found anything convincing we could say, have we?"

As soon as the nomination was a done deed, whether it went for Humphrey or not, our client, United Democrats for Humphrey, would go out of business. The new client organization for the candidate would be the Democratic National Committee.

Meanwhile, with only two days of life left in the UDH, more and more flies gathered about the corpse-to-be. All of our ads and commericals now had to be screened by Lloyd Wright and his group; Senator Harris (Mondale had vanished somewhere along the way); Napolitan; O'Brien; Jeno Paulucci; Julie Cahn; Short and the Citizens Group; and a new entry, ex-Secretary of Agriculture Orville Freeman, whom we had met once before in our conference in Humphrey's Washington offices. Each of them firmly believed that he was to be the final judge of what would be presented to Humphrey.

We discussed all this with Lloyd. Bernbach told him firmly that we had to have one client, only one, or nothing would ever get produced.

"I agree," Lloyd said, "but we're only talking about two days. After that, you've got to get ready to pitch the real client, the Democratic National Committee. And you'll be doing it against competition. You know that Lennon & Newell has been working for them for a while now, and they have a lot of friends in court."

Bernbach told him icily that we had no intention of pitching against any agency, much less (with contempt) Lennon & Newell. "They have done nothing but junk posters, junk brochures, and junk mailers," he said.

"There are a lot of people in this business who set a great store by junk," Lloyd replied.

I followed this discussion wearily. Not only did we not have an account as yet, much less a single strong client, but I had come to feel that we did not even have a candidate. There seemed to be no Hubert Horatio Humphrey; each advisory group had removed a piece of the real man.

Amazingly, we continued to work. All of us were churning out storyboards around the clock, just as if there was a real need for them. Most of the work was right-wing "Law and Order" stuff, designed to attract Wallace voters. "Law and Order" was, at that time, code for Anti-Black, Anti-Liberal, Anti-Young, and Anti-Poor. It represented everything that each of us was personally opposed to, but the polls showed what the public wanted to hear; and if we didn't tell them what they wanted to hear, Humphrey wouldn't stand a chance.

Politics is the art of the possible.

On the 28th of August, the last day of the convention, only hours before Humphrey would be nominated, we met with Jeno, Lloyd, and Dennis. Bernbach presented twenty-five storyboards, carefully culled from a stack of thirty-seven.

The twelve not presented dealt with a wide variety of issues, but not with "Law and Order."

Only one of the twenty-five presented boards did *not* deal with "Law and Order." Eventually it would be the only one to be produced and aired.

The morning after the nomination, I woke up tired and ill. I couldn't rid myself of the TV images of the night before:

the bleeding kids, the beaten newsmen, the howling and charging cops. Could anyone have dreamed a fantasy like the festival of hate in the streets? Could anyone have imagined a fantasy like a major political figure speaking out against long hair and sideburns to the assembled delegates in the convention hall?

I turned on the TV to hear what the commentators had to say. What I got was Humphrey himself being interviewed by Hugh Downs on the "Today" show. Downs was sickened, and he asked Humphrey to say a few words about the violence.

Humphrey spoke with no shock, no horror, no compassion, and no humanity. He gave a little lecture on the right way and wrong way to protest, pointing out that the kids, after all, were out there looking for trouble.

"You just had to look at them," he said reasonably. "They came prepared for trouble. They were wearing helmets."

No matter how you say that sentence, there is no way you can make a helmet sound like a weapon.

I decided I would do no more advertising for Humphrey.

It took me only a few days after returning to New York to decide that I wanted to do no more advertising for Bill Bernbach, either. He had treated me no worse than he had treated Ken, Lee, Paula, Norm, Bob, Ed, Arie, or Bruce. But I was at a point where I was unable to accept it any longer.

On Friday, September 13, I came in to pick up my final paycheck, arrange to have my books and papers shipped to Papert Koenig Lois, and to say goodbye to my friends.

The goodbyes were different this time than in my previous departures from DDB. This time, I had become a sort of folk hero to the younger creative staff. Kids I hardly even knew came to see me and say embarrassing things like, "Proud to shake your hand."

Just before noon, as I was about to go to lunch with David Larson and never to return, Ken called me to say that we had just been fired from the Humphrey account. The agency was Lennon & Newell, which I had once dubbed "last agency before the turnpike."

TRAVELING ON

George Lois had left PKL less than a year before to start his second agency, Lois Holland Calloway.

He had explained that ever since the agency had taken an assignment from Procter & Gamble a few years earlier, the whole place had become dominated by P&G mentalities. He didn't say that a P&G mentality was a bad thing to have, but he did say that it was not a fun thing to have, "and if advertising isn't any fun, why do it?"

Of course he was right, and of course I should have paid attention. George always was in things for the fun, and although he had become rich in the business, he never acted as if that was the important thing.

I remembered when PKL went public, the first agency to ever do so. In the initial stock offering, George had made a million dollars. I read this in the prospectus and then called and asked him to meet me for a drink. "Sure," he said. "Let's meet in the saloon downstairs in my building."

The saloon downstairs was the Four Seasons bar. George pulled a stool close to me and asked what I had in mind. I told him I had nothing in mind except to buy him a drink, because I had never bought a drink for a millionaire.

George said very seriously, "I'm not a millionaire."

I told him I had read the prospectus and knew exactly what he was worth.

"Sure, but you don't understand," he said. "A millionaire isn't a guy who's worth a million dollars. It's a guy whose money *earns* a million dollars."

He was only about twenty-seven years old then. He already knew all about money and wasn't the least impressed by it.

Now he was off on his own, looking for more fun, and the money be damned, and I was joining what had been his agency, where he had publicly said that the fun had stopped.

That's what I thought about as I went to work for the first time at PKL, no longer in the Seagram building but at 777 Third Avenue. I went straight in to see Fred Papert, and after he'd finished welcoming me, I told him what was on my mind.

"Precisely why we want you here," he said. "I think you can put some of the fun, the spirit, back into this place."

"Maybe when I recover," I said, "but right now, don't ask me to do more than make good advertising. After the last few months, my fun quotient has gone down pretty low on the scale."

Fred told me not to worry about it. He'd known me a long time, since our Sudler & Hennessey days, and he knew I'd bounce right back, as soon as I was working on a fun account.

The one account I had my eye on was Bromo Seltzer, a nearly moribund brand that spent very little on advertising. It looked to me to be a great creative opportunity, if I could only figure out what to do with it. This was at the time of the early great Alka Seltzer commercials from Wells Rich Green, created by Gene Case and Bob Wilvers, and I wanted nothing better than a chance to give them some competition in the fizzy antacid category.

Fred said sure, take the account and good luck. But I also had to take on National Airlines. Okay, you pay for what you want, one way or another.

The problem with Bromo Seltzer was that it had so small an ad budget that whatever one did for it would be among the best kept secrets of the year. The only way I could see to get frequency and awareness was to produce only one ten-second TV spot and run it heavily on the late shows where the audience for hangover cures was creating its need for the morning's fizzy fix.

What I came up with was a spot featuring Dean Martin. He was to do his familiar, slightly tottering walk towards the camera with that gesture of his, lightly touching his temple with the fingers of his right hand. All he had to do was to sing the opening of his theme song, "Everybody needs somebody sometime," with a slight lyric change: "Everybody needs a Bromo sometime." Cut to black with the Bromo Seltzer logo and a pack shot.

"Brilliant!" said Fred. "A sure-fire award winner!" said Monte. "It'll put the brand on the map!" said the account guy.

"No way," said the client.

Bromo Seltzer was a family-owned business. The family were conservative, God-fearing, fundamentalist Christians, opposed to alcohol and anything connected with drinking. They refused to allow their brand to be positioned as a hangover cure. Never mind that what little awareness of the brand existed was as a hangover cure.

"What do they think it *is* for?" I asked.

"Acid indigestion, mostly from eating too much," the client said.

I came back a few days later with a new spot. It was Dean Martin again, doing the same thing as before, only this time instead of singing, he was to say, "Boy, did I over . . . eat last night."

"Get out of here with that drunk and don't come back again," said the client.

My other fun account was National Airlines, and the campaign I had to work with was summed up by a pretty actress named Andrea Dromm who, dressed as a stewardess (flight attendants hadn't been invented yet) ended each commercial by saying, "Is that any way to run an airline? You bet it is!"

I learned on my first shoot with Andrea that she could say that line perfectly, just the way she had always said it, but she couldn't say it any other way. Worse, she couldn't say anything else.

I immediately created a new campaign that kept the line, but got rid of Andrea.

The idea was to create a weekly commercial for each of National's eleven major destinations. Each one would be a guide to what was going on in that city that week. For each city we would have a theme song, its only common thread being the end line, "Is that any way to run an airline: You bet it is!"

It sounds complex, and it was. But it was doable, and the client agreed that it was worth doing. We figured to put most of our money in radio, back it up with a little TV and with a lot of promotional activities, such as a "This Week in Miami" flyer (or New York or New Orleans or wherever) to be handed out to each boarding passenger.

I wrote lyrics for theme songs for Miami, New Orleans, and New York for examples. I decided that Hoagy Carmichael would be the perfect composer and lyricist for the whole package. His agent was intrigued, and Hoagy agreed. We spoke on the phone for an hour at a time, reworking my lyrics and actually keeping most of the original words and rhymes. I still can hardly believe that happened.

And then, just as everyone was happy, reality hit the fan.

Our Talent Payment Department told us that the residual payments for the jingle singers would cost more than the whole production budget. You see, each time we inserted a new weekly announcement into the jingle's donut, the singers would have to get paid a new session fee. If we advertised 40 weeks out of the year in 11 cities, we would have to pay each of five singers 440 session fees, for a total of 2,200 session fees.

A session fee wasn't much at the time, maybe about $225.

But even at that, it added up to $99,000 a singer, or a total of $495,000.

There was no way around it, according to Talent Payments.

There was no way he'd pay for it, said Al Gilmore, National's Advertising Manager. With deep regrets he asked me to go back to the drawing board and come up with a new campaign.

Instead, John Capsis, who headed Telpac, a company that acted as Production Department for PKL and other agencies, came up with a solution.

"We'll record it in London and buy out the talent," he said. "There are plenty of singers there who can do American accents; you'll never hear the difference."

We needed an excuse to give the union for recording abroad. If we were shooting abroad, they'd allow it. But this was radio.

"Easy," John said. "We want a particular voice-over talent who is in Europe now on vacation and who won't interrupt her vacation to come back for a recording session."

"But I know who I want for the voice-overs," I said. "It's Terry Keane, and she's right here in New York."

"She won't be when we need her," John said.

That's how Terry Keane got a paid vacation in Europe, broken only by a few working days in London. And that's how John Capsis, Account Supervisor Mike Reingold, Ellen, and I got to be the first people I ever heard of to go abroad for a music session.

The music, arranged and conducted by Cliff Adams, was terrific. The singers were perfectly American. And then we did one version just for Al Gilmore, who was sure he'd be able to hear an English accent. It was straight American until the last line when the singers went into broad Cockney with "Is that any wy t'run an airloin? You bet yer arse!"

So we were having fun again. And we kept on having fun for a few months until PKL became the first agency ever to be fired by Procter, which brought on more account losses and a widespread belief that the agency was going down the drain. Whenever that feeling gets around, there's only one thing to do—give up and let the agency go down the drain.

When I left, PKL was making gurgling noises.

TRAVELING FURTHER ON

David McCall had asked me several times to come to work for him at McCaffery & McCall. Since there was no place in particular that I wanted to work, and no reason not to work at McC & McC, I phoned him before taking the train home and asked if he still wanted me. He told me I couldn't have picked a better time and asked me to come in to work the next morning.

"Hadn't you better tell me what you have in mind?" I asked cautiously.

"It's an assignment just made for you," David said. "And to make it even better, you'll be working with Cliff Field."

That made it (whatever it was) nearly irresistible, as McCall had known it would.

The next morning, over coffee, we settled the salary matter quickly (I was back up to $60,000 again) and moved on to the job David wanted me to do. It was a hell of a job, and it did seem to be just made for me.

Standard Oil of New Jersey, otherwise known as Esso (Exxon hadn't been invented yet) had its corporate account with McCaffery & McCall. Cliff had been creating a handsome series of ads for them that told of the care SONJ took in all their operations not to damage the environment by oil spills, air pollution, visual messes, or any other means. The target audience for this message was small enough so that the client and agency knew them all by name. They were the members of Congress, of regulatory bodies, and environmental groups such as the Sierra Club. The ads were never intended to win the hearts and minds of these people (nobody was that naive), but rather to forestall restrictive legislation by saying, in effect, "Hey, guys, go easy on us; we're already trying to do the best we can."

Where I came in was where Cliff had backed off. TV had been chosen as the better way to get at the audience, and Cliff had never been comfortable with TV. He would keep right on with the print campaign, and I would create film equivalents for it.

To find the right stories and shoot them, I would travel all around the world. David and Cliff felt that my experience at DDB Germany, shooting in foreign countries, and in many languages around Europe would be invaluable. I agreed and was excited by the prospect.

There was one problem with the plan. The decision had been made to create a Sunday evening news program that would be sponsored solely by SONJ. Because there was no Sunday evening news at the time, it was believed that all the people they wanted to reach would tune in so as to be on top of things at the start of Monday's political day. What made this a problem was that SONJ had never made a commercial and wanted not to repeat one in any evening's show. We would need three one-minute spots in the first half hour, three more a week later, and so on for a month. Then, they felt, we could start to recycle commercials while creating new ones at a more orderly pace.

The show, anchored by Roger Mudd, was due for its first airing on CBS in less than three months.

Somehow we did it.

Working with several art directors, including Fred Peterkin and David Stickles, and sometimes working without one, I wrote almost all the copy. I brought John Capsis and Telpac into the picture because we knew we would need anywhere from three to five producers on the job.

I covered most of the shoots. Each one required two trips: the first to research the story to see if it was worth telling in film, and if so how to tell it, and the second to do the filming.

For the next year I was away from home for more than half the time, and only occasionally was Ellen able to come with me. It damn near broke up our marriage.

We shot in Venezuela, in Alaska, in Holland, in the Northwest Passage above the Arctic Circle. We shot in Australia; underwater in the Bahamas; on the King Ranch in Texas; on Avery Island in Louisiana where Tabasco Sauce comes from; in Benicia, California; Harlem, N.Y.; on a shrimp boat in the Gulf of Mexico; and in a refinery on Aruba. We shot in a shipyard in Newcastle-Upon-Tyne and in another one on the Mississippi north of New Orleans.

In all, we shot more than twenty commercials during that exhausting, stimulating, exciting, and nearly disastrous year.

When it was all over, David McCall came to my seldom-used office to talk to me.

He told me that the client was delighted with the work, felt that all of the commercials were so interesting they could be viewed many times, and that they, therefore, had enough in the can to take them on for at least a year before they would have to produce any more.

"Fine," I said. "I've had enough travel to last me a lifetime. What have you got for me to work on?"

"Nothing," David said. "That is, nothing that would merit what we're paying you. So I'm afraid I'll have to let you go."

He then went on to give me a little lesson in agency economics, explaining that a four million dollar account only netted an agency about $60,000.

"So you see," he said reasonably, "firing you is as good as getting a four million dollar account."

I couldn't argue with that.

Feeling slightly raped, I started to work out what I ought to do next.

MY NAME ON A DOOR

It was June of 1970. The country was having its first major recession since the end of World War II. Advertisers were cutting back on their budgets, the average production cost for a commercial fell in a matter of months from $35,000 to a reported $12,000, and a lot of scared marketers were taking their advertising in-house.

It seemed to me like a great time to open my own agency.

I reasoned that in a time like that, old loyalties would be dropped, old habits of thought would be broken, and advertisers would open their minds to new ways of doing things if they thought they might save a buck in the process.

I wanted an account man for a partner. I talked to some of the best I had worked with, and most of them thought I was right in my timing, but none was willing to leave a safe harbor to venture into the economic storm. I couldn't blame them either, as I wouldn't be doing this myself if I still had a job.

I found my partner in the person of John McManus. I had worked with him at DDB when he was Account Supervisor on Avis, Mobile Oil, and Rainier Beer. John, a dark-haired Irishman with the red nose and chops of a steady drinker, had never appeared to me as a tower of strength or a font of wisdom, but we had gotten along well enough. He had an affable manner, responded well to good advertising ideas, and if he never seemed to move matters ahead, he also never got in the way.

We met by chance on the train platform in Westport. We rode in together and talked about the possibility of teaming up. John was all full of enthusiasm, but with one condition: we would have to start our agency in Westport, not in New York, for his own pressing and quite real personal reasons. It was a new thought for me, and I wasn't sure I liked it, but I told him I'd think about it and get back to him in a week.

The more I thought about it, the more I liked it. I had been away from home so much in the last year that my kids were calling me "Uncle Daddy," and Ellen was calling me all kinds of rotten things. Working in the town I lived in would give me a chance to spend more time with them and maybe straighten things out between us all.

From a business point of view, I thought I could make a sensible pitch out of the location, especially since I thought our best prospects would not be in New York. What could it matter to a client in Ohio or Missouri where our offices were?

I had enough money to pay half the start-up costs, such as office space, a secretary, stationery, phones, and a copier, plus enough to live on for nine months. We had no clients and no immediate prospects, and I figured if we didn't get a good client in six months, we could always close up, and I could look for a job while I still had three months' living in the bank.

We opened Herzbrun, McManus & Co. on July 1. About ten days later, before our business cards had come back from the printer, we had our first new business presentation. My old friend Aaron Burns was advising his old friend and schoolmate, Frank Lautenberg (Senator Lautenberg hadn't been invented yet), on selecting an agency for his company, Automatic Data Processing, now called ADP. The agency review was supposedly completed, but when Aaron heard that I was in business, he called Lautenberg and insisted that we be given a hearing.

It was a $3 million account, a bigger chance than we had dreamed of. It would put us in business in a very profitable way, starting in our first month.

We met at ADP's offices in New Jersey and enthusiastically expounded our ideas on what we could do for them. We didn't have a chart, a slide, or a leave-behind piece.

When we finished, Lautenberg said the magic words that I had never before and have never since heard following a new business pitch: "You've got the account."

Then he added, "Provided you stop this Connecticut nonsense. I want you to set up in New York."

It was no use explaining that we could be in New Jersey faster than we could be in Manhattan. He wanted to be able to visit his agency from time to time, and he didn't want to drive to Connecticut.

I think now that if the ADP account had been offered to us four or five months later, I would have gone to New York for it and left McManus behind to deal with his problems at home. But it had come so easily that I was sure the next account would be just as much of a cinch to get.

We passed it up, and Lautenberg picked another brand-new agency—Scali, McCabe & Sloves.

For the next five months, we didn't get so much as a nibble.

I filled my time by writing door-opener letters (they opened very few doors) in the mornings and by following up on letters previously sent. In the afternoons I tried to write a novel.

Toward the end of July, I got a call from my ex-partner, Ken Duskin, asking me if I would like to work with him on Nelson Rockefeller's fourth campaign for governor of New York. Ken was working at the time for what remained of Jack Tinker & Partners as co-Creative Director with Marcella Free, and Marcella didn't feel comfortable or competent working in politics.

After the Humphrey mess, I didn't feel comfortable either, but I did feel competent. And besides, I needed the money.

We did some good work in the next months, creating ads and commercials that won some nice awards and that may have done something to help Rockefeller win his final term as governor of New York state.

Rockefeller was good to work with: genial, tough, smart, a quick study. I liked him a lot, until after the election.

That's when he started doing everything we had promised he wouldn't do. And doing none of the things we promised he would. I understood, of course. Politics is the art of the possible. Had he promised his real program, he wouldn't have gotten elected. But I still felt like a paid liar and it was a feeling I had never liked.

Anyway, the money came in handy.

Our first account came in six months, almost to the day, from our opening, just as I was preparing to start looking for a job.

It was Monsanto's corporate business, awarded to us by Eric Erickson, who was heading up the Monsanto in-house advertising operation. All we got was the creative work, no account service or media placement, but we were allowed to announce the appointment as agency of record and to list the account in the *Red Book*.

Suddenly we were taken seriously by accounts we had been wooing fecklessly for months. Even Bill Bernback took us seriously, recommending us to a company in which he was an investor and a board member.

The company, Videorecord Corporation of America, was to be a national chain of franchised videocassette distributors. It was seriously ahead of its time. Even though they planned to limit their efforts for the first years to training programs for business and industry, schools and hospitals, it was still almost impossible to buy a video playback unit and completely impossible to buy a reliable one.

Our job was to create advertising that would sell the very expensive franchises that were to be the corporation's main source of revenue.

Unfortunately, we did it too well. Our first ad produced such a deluge of applications for franchises that the company could barely process them. All further advertising was stopped.

All we got out of it by the time that Videorecord went belly-up was a first in the New England Hatch Awards, a few distinguished merits in other shows, and an Effie. But that was all we needed to give us speed.

Two and a half years later we had a staff, our own impressive building, billings of nearly $7 million, and a list of blue-chip clients. In addition to Monsanto Corporate, we had been assigned their Acrilan and Nylon fibers business. We had Alfa Romeo; the housing division of Bethlehem Steel; assignments from General Foods; Godiva Chocolates, and gourmet specialties from Pepperidge Farm; plus a few more small but promising accounts.

It was all going wonderfully, and I hated it.

I hated being an agency President and having too little time to write advertising. I hated dealing with accountants, bankers, and lawyers. I hated worrying about personnel problems, cash flow, getting and keeping tenants for our oversized Greek Revival building; there was nothing about it that I liked.

To make matters worse, I also hated John McManus.

Ours had been from the start a marriage of convenience, not a romance. It is not unusual for such arrangements to create unforeseen difficulties.

We had been dumb enough to set up the business as a fifty-fifty partnership. McManus refused to sell me his stock or to buy mine.

So I quit.

I took the Monsanto business with me, because they wanted me to keep writing their ads. I left everything else, nearly $6 million worth, with the agency, because I didn't want an agency any more and John did.

To give him credit, he kept it going for almost three years before going bankrupt. I would never had bet on it.

BETWEEN ROLES

I rented office space, secretarial services, and the use of the copier from Weston Group, a marketing services company housed next door to my ex-agency's mansion in what looked like the caretaker's cottage.

Jack Lewis, the President of Weston Group, had become a good friend in the past couple of years. We had hoped to find some way to work together and were sure that we'd have some opportunties with me on the premises.

I worked happily on Monsanto Corporate, doing it easily by now after nearly three years. On my occasional trips to their headquarters in St. Louis, where I toured their many different divisions in search of corporate stories, I was accepted as a member of their family.

Acrilan was becoming an interesting and amusing piece of business too, largely because of its Advertising Manager, John Bunbury. John was a lively, funny, and very smart man who had been a friend of mine since the days when he had been my client at DDB on the old Chemstrand business.

Weston Group did, indeed, find use for my services, and in turn I found use for theirs. Jack became my partner on Monsanto whenever smart marketing thinking was needed.

And then there were the surprises, the pieces of business that just came in, as they say, over the transom.

Transoms show up in funny places. My favorite one was in a phone booth in Brattleboro, Vermont.

Ellen and I were taking a vacation, and I called the office every day to check on messages. The message that day was an

173

urgent request to call a man at Chase Manhattan Bank in New York.

I called and spoke to a pleasant man who would rather not have his name used in this story. He said that he was looking for ideas for a new corporate advertising campaign, had greatly admired the Monsanto work, and had called them to find out who was doing it. He asked if I could come in to see him the next day to be briefed on an assignment.

I explained that I was on vacation and asked if it couldn't wait a week, but was assured that it couldn't. He offered me $1,000 just to pay for the inconvenience if I would come in right away, whether or not I accepted the assignment. It was impossible to say no.

The assignment was unusual. It was the client's hope to find a corporate campaign he liked that he could give to his agency, Ted Bates.

Bates, he explained, was doing a fine job on the retail part of the account, but was completely unable to come up with an idea for corporate. They had tried nine times, and each time were further from the mark. Did I mind, the client asked, that I would not have a chance to execute the advertising and would never have a chance for an ongoing relationship with Chase?

No, I didn't mind, as long as it paid okay.

His next question was whether I minded that he had already hired another creative group (he thought I was a group), and I would be in competition with them.

No, I assured him, that made no difference to me as long as he paid for my time.

His last question, of course, was how much it was going to cost him. I had been considering this while we'd been talking and had figured I could do the job in five working days at $500 a day, plus $500 for an art director to do some rough layouts. Add another day for contact time and the total would be $3,500.

Instead of saying so, something made me say, "I'll take whatever you're paying the other group." "That's fair," he said, "and probably generous. I'm paying them $10,000. Are you sure that's all right?"

"A deal's a deal," I said reluctantly, "so I'll stand by my offer."

I finished the job in two days, stalled for ten more to make it look right, delivered the work (my client and his associates were delighted) and handed in my bill.

Two days later, a check for $10,000 came in the mail.

I brought it home and showed it to Ellen. "Do you know what this is?" I said. "It is not money. It's a boat."

We bought a 26-foot cruising sailboat and named it Chase.

One day Paccione called. "Dorfsman says you're free-lancing. I really need a good writer. Can you come in to see me?"

Patch had sold out his interest in Leber Katz Paccione and had a loose arrangement with a faltering agency called Clyne Maxon, owned by an endangered species named Terry Clyne. He had a suite of offices, a retainer, a gorgeous secretary, and a business partner named Guy Shea.

Their idea was to build a creative boutique, not an agency, that would serve clients and agencies alike, and they really needed a third partner.

I loved the idea of working with Patch, but I wasn't at all excited about commuting to New York every day. The three of us went to lunch at Capriccio on 56th Street, where Patch had a permanent table, and after enough wine (there is always enough wine when you dine with Patch) I gave in part of the way.

We agreed to start a new company with the eclectic name of Paccione, Herzbrun & Shea. I would continue to keep my own business in Connecticut and come to New York only twice a week on a scheduled basis and more if we had a real need.

Patch designed exquisite stationery and business cards, Shea got out the appropriate press releases, and two weeks later we were making new business calls.

Guy Shea was a smoothly charming man who talked and looked like one of the Kennedys. He had gone to a pretty good prep school where he got the right manners and accent to match his looks. He was good at opening doors and closing deals. He and Patch had come to know each other when Shea had been a public relations man specializing in PR for ad agencies.

He claimed to have put Wells Rich Green on the map as well

as Papert Koenig Lois, Leber Katz Paccione, and a few other hot creative shops that I had always thought put themselves on the map with their work and awards.

Much to my surprise, Guy actually brought in business. We did campaigns for a few out-of-town agencies, new product work for General Electric, projects for others. A London headhunter named Rosie Oxley set up dates for me with English agencies, convinced as I was that I could sell the American magic abroad.

One of my first visits was at a small creative boutique called Saatchi & Saatchi. At that time, early 1974, they had just begun to emerge as a hot new creative shop worth watching. I don't believe their staff numbered more than a dozen. I was received pleasantly, if a little shyly, by Charles Saatchi, a curly-haired and very young man. He gave me coffee and showed me his agency's work with a neat mixture of pride and diffidence.

The work was very good. It was Doyle Dane Bernbach of the 60s with an extra flash of sly British wit. I told him that any pitch I could make would clearly be of no use, that he had no need for Patch and me. With evident relief he agreed.

I asked Charles where he had learned to do work like that, and he told me with no hesitation that whenever he was up against it for an idea, he would open up some New York awards annuals and shop for an inspiration. He had become a thoroughly knowledgeable observer of the New York ad world, familiar with all of Patch's work and my own.

As we parted, I said I was sure his agency would go far.

But as for what happened, it never entered my mind.

I returned to New York with promises of work from other, duller agencies who needed us. During my travels, the workload from Clyne Maxon increased dramatically, as Terry Clyne found himself at risk of losing GE, which would put him out of business. We were doing very well financially.

I still can't believe what happened next.

Unknown to Patch and me, Guy talked an officer at Chemical Bank, where we had our account, into giving us a corporate loan of $300,000. The law requires the signature of two officers for such a loan, but Shea somehow got the man to go along with him. He had the money deposited to our account, and two days later withdrew the entire amount and vanished. Absconded. Without a trace.

The bank fired the officer, held Patch and me harmless in the matter, and called Interpol. Just like in a cheap novel.*

In a cheap novel, Patch and I would have found Shea and killed him. In real life, even Interpol didn't find him.

Clyne Maxon lost GE, so we lost our retainer and our office space. We spent a lot of money paying outstanding bills from suppliers, had a last lunch at Capriccio, and went out of business.

It had lasted about a year, and it sure had been fun while it lasted.

As we came out of Capriccio I saw Nelson Rockefeller getting out of his limousine. I turned the other way to avoid a run-in, but he was too fast for me.

"David!" he called. "Come say hello."

So I said hello.

"What's the matter? Are you mad at me?" He looked puzzled.

"Yes," I told him, "because you made me a paid liar."

He laughed, "I thought you were a pro."

"No," I said. "I'm not a pro. Not in politics; not in advertising. I'm an amateur. I'm in it only for a good time."

---

*Guy Shea was never apprehended by police and was never convicted of any crime. If he reads this and comes forward, he might possibly exonerate himself with a good explanation of what happened.

IN THE TIME MACHINE

After the collapse of PKL, my friend Mike Reingold, who had been Account Supervisor on National Airlines, joined Lois Holland Calloway and later left them and tried another thing or two, finally deciding to return to his native Boston to work for an agency called Ingalls Associates.

Mike and I kept in pretty close touch during those years. At one point, he had introduced McManus and me to Joe Hoffman, co-owner of Ingalls, to start a series of finally fruitless discussions about a possible merger.

Joe didn't want to merge or to acquire us, but he did try at the time, and several times later, to get me to quit and come to work for him in Boston.

Now, on the collapse of Paccione, Herzbrun & Shea, he and Mike got back in touch and asked again. This time I agreed.

I joined Ingalls in the fall of 1974. My arrival in Boston made banner headlines (no kidding) in the local trade publication. Everyone wanted to meet me, and there were parties and lunches with agency folks from all over town. It was very exciting for me, and just a little scary.

All those nice people had a great opinion of me based on their careful reading of old advertising awards annuals. But that work had been done in the 60s, and the 60s were already a legend, and this was a different time.

Except in Boston.

In Boston, it was still the 50s, and everyone knew that their 60s were in sight. They were eager for their own creative revolution and more than ready to take their places on the barricades.

It was already happening at Humphrey Browning Mac-Dougall and, in a pun-rudden, fumbling manner at Hill Holliday Connors Cosmopulos. Joe and Mike wanted it to happen in the best professional way at Ingalls.

I knew that I would have to do the work on some account myself, as well as be Creative Director of the agency, in order to let the agency (and the rest of Boston) see that I could do it, that I wasn't a burned-out case who had left New York because I couldn't get a job.

I waited for a nice new piece of business to come in for me, as I couldn't take an account away from one of my writers. The first thing to come in, about a week after I started, was Michael Dukakis's first run for governor of Massachusetts.

This was not the account I wanted. My recent chat with Nelson Rockefeller had recalled everything I didn't like about politicians and had left a taste like iodine in my mouth. The agency management, especially Harold Turin, who 'was a close friend of Dukakis's and would be Management Supervisor on the business, wanted me to do the work.

I met with Dukakis and his wife at their home and found him to be a most articulate, intelligent, and attractive man. As he talked about what his program would be, I found myself wanting to work for him. In the end, I kept some distance by promising to supervise everything closely, but managed to avoid actual work by pleading ignorance of Massachusetts politics.

I hired a wonderful writer named Bob Baker, left him pretty much alone, and got unearned credit for a winning campaign.

My personal account, my showcase, was a new furniture store in Braintree, a brilliantly staged fantasy called Hamilton's. I decided to take on the newspaper part of the account and write three or more full-page ads a week, many of them long copy. I had a wonderful time doing it.

I looked in from time to time on the rest of the work the agency was doing, but didn't have to give much to it. I had a talented staff, and I dealt with them on the old DDB maxim that the best supervision is the least supervision.

In the spring, at the Hatch Awards, we got our scorecard.

We had done extremely well. I personally won a good collection of cups and satisfied Boston's doubts about whether I was an extinct volcano. But there were two great surprises, including the one sorry disappointment.

The good news was that the agency had taken the first prize for TV with a campaign for a local broadcaster. It was a good campaign, but even its creators thought it didn't deserve a first. That honor should have gone to Humphrey Browning Mac-Dougall for their outstanding work on Parker Brothers Games, A&W Root Beer, or Titleist Golf Balls.

The bad news was that Hamilton's didn't take the first prize for newspaper. It went, instead, to HBM for some fairly ordinary but workmanlike campaign that I've since forgotten.

The minute the show was over, I ran out to the lobby to find Mal MacDougall to tell him how embarrassed I was to have had Ingalls take the first in TV. I found him looking for me to tell me how wrong it was for Hamilton's not to have won the first in newspaper.

We made a date for lunch when we could have time to bitch more extensively about the vicissitudes of awards juries.

We had such a good time at lunch that it was impossible not to accept the job offer that accompanied the coffee.

And there I was, whisked back in time to something very like DDB in the late 50s.

There was an energy, an esprit de corps, a feeling of being one of a chosen few, blessed with talent, youth (even I felt that, although I was forty-eight at the time) and singled out by the Gods for some special and delightful fate.

A lot of this energy came straight from MacDougall, a man who seemed incapable of moderation. Every new campaign concept ever brought to him was either "Fabulous! Brilliant! *Wonn*-derful!" or "The worst piece of garbage I've ever seen; a disaster; horrible."

He seemed so low, so beaten, so *betrayed* when bad work (by whatever standards he was applying that day) was brought to him that everyone made every effort to keep his spirits buoyed up by creating exciting new ideas for him.

Everyone on that creative staff loved Mal, and he used that love to great effect, as Bernbach had used fear. And for a few years, we actually became as good as we thought we were.

What gives an agency this magical quality is more than the sum of its parts, more than the quality of its leaders and their abilities to inspire. I am convinced that the one essential is a shared sense of mission. We had it at DDB: a need to prove that the audience was not stupid, that wit (and sometimes humor) could sell products, and that the greatest gimmick was the truth.

At HBM our mission was to show that Boston could create advertising equal to anything that came out of New York.

Mal MacDougall had, at first, positioned HBM as "Boston's New York Agency," a battle cry that was not heard outside the walls of the city, but that gave the place an internal point of view about itself and that worked very well against New England clients. But now we were ready to move on, to make a name for the agency on the national scene. We never did write a slogan for this phase, but it could nearly have been "New York's Boston Agency," as Fallon McElligott years later became New York's Minneapolis agency.

I had told Mal at that first lunch that I would come to work for him providing that I could just be a copywriter, with no supervisory responsibilities. He agreed, but insisted that I be given a Senior Vice Presidency, a seat on the Board of Directors and the title of Associate Creative Director. This was a bigger title then than it is now. Mal was Creative Director, and nobody held the title of Associate.

I didn't like it. It boded ill.

Mal assured me that he was only doing it so that he could justify my salary to Humphrey and Browning, who still owned the vast majority of the stock. They would never put up with paying a mere copywriter the embarrassingly large sum, plus company car, that I had accepted without negotiation.

I got a lovely corner office with a view over the State House's gold dome, of Beacon Hill, Back Bay, and Cambridge across the Charles River. From the other windows, I could see Boston's new Civic Center area and beyond it to the inner harbor, Charlestown and, on especially clear days, up the coast to Cape Ann.

I felt as if I owned it all.

My partner was Mary Moore, a witty, exciting, brilliant, provocative advertising thinker and art director, and to top it all, an immensely attractive woman.

Mary will call that last comment old-fashioned male chauvinist piggery. Come off it, Mary.

We worked as a team on Parker Brothers games and toys and had a wonderful time bringing the games' fantasies to life in a series of commercials, perhaps a dozen a year, that were mostly fun to produce and almost always fun to watch.

We also worked on A&W Root Beer, creating a group of spots that had nothing to do with conventional soft drink advertising.

We assembled a nice collection of the little silver Revere bowls that are the Hatch Awards and also began taking prizes in the New York shows.

By 1977, HBM took more awards in the New York shows than any other agency except Doyle Dane Bernbach, which was more than ten times our size and submitted more than twenty times the number of our entries.

And then the inevitable happened; the MBAs took over.

Parker Brothers, which had been a nice group of people who liked to create and play games and who had a collective well-developed sense of fantasy, had been sold in 1975 to General Mills, which promised to let the company run as it always had, with no interference.

By 1978, Parker Brothers no longer resembled the old family business, but was run by humorless men who had learned their lessons in packaged-goods companies. To them, there was no difference between selling a game or a cereal. Both were just "a box of product," as one of them told me.

A game is no more a box of product than is a movie or a book. A game is entertainment, and often fantasy. The fantasy—not the hardware, the board, or the play—is what made

Monopoly the most successful game in history. The fantasy of owning railroads, utilities, hotels was a heady one when the game was introduced in the depths of the Great Depression. The new games, too, all carried their own load of wish fulfillment and cloud candy.

Go explain that to an MBA in a white shirt.

I spent a lot of time in New York during those years. We did most of our TV production there, and I was on the Shuttle two or three days a week.

One morning while breakfasting at the Edwardian Room (I always stayed at the Plaza; we were its ad agency), I read in the *Times* that both Bill Bernbach and David Ogilvy were to be inducted into the Advertising Hall of Fame at a luncheon that day at the Waldorf.

I was free for lunch and decided to show up and see if there was a spare ticket. I arrived early to get my best shot and was reluctantly sold a ticket to sit with a mixed bag at a table at the far fringe of the hall.

I was alone in the antechamber to the ballroom, pinning on my name tag, when David showed up unaccompanied. He was given his (quite unnecessary) badge, and I went over to say hello and pin it on for him. It had been nearly a dozen years since we had spoken, but his greeting was as casual as if it had been yesterday and as warm as if it had been fifty years.

We had not talked for more than a few minutes when Bill arrived. He hurried over to join us, not bothering to stop for a name tag. He, too, made time disappear by greeting me as if I were still working for him and as if he were only wondering who had invited me.

"How did you ever let this man get away from you?" Ogilvy asked.

"You stole him from me," Bernbach replied.

"And you stole him back," David said.

"Yes, I did," Bill said calmly and triumphantly.

Both of them were wrong, but neither knew it. Each had reshaped history to suit his own story, in which he was the hero, the central figure about whom all action revolves and without whom no action would occur. My motivations, my feelings, had no part in their stories.

And as I remember this, I realize that their motivations, their feelings, have no part in my story. I can only assume that I, too, am refashioning the facts to suit my own purposes, though I try my best to remember what really did happen.

One thing I am sure of is what happened that day, the last day, by chance, that I saw David Ogilvy. I am sure becasue the observation that sticks in my memory was not made by me, but by an unforgettable stranger.

Bill Bernbach, courtesy of the alphabet, spoke first.

It was a familiar speech, the same basic speech that he had been making for years, since before the birth of DDB, since the days when he was copy chief at Grey. Bill never needed a new speech; he had always known what he believed in and what had to be said again and again. And yet, as familiar as that address was to him, he could never say it without a script. He read his revolutionary, inflammatory words that condemned the idea of "scientific advertising" and hailed our craft as an art in dry, dispassionate tones that carried none of the conviction he felt. His was the manner of a CPA approaching the bottom line of a tax return not his own.

At the bottom line, the audience responded with a strong round of applause as Bill Bernbach was inducted into the Advertising Hall of Fame.

And then, David Ogilvy took the podium.

He spoke, as always, without notes. I have no idea of what he said because he had no set speech. I don't think he was trying to convince the lunchers of anything; he was only trying to make love to them. He was very good at it.

When the thunderous applause died down, a young woman who had been sitting next to me leaned toward me and grasped my arm.

"Wasn't that fabulous?" she said. "I'll never forget today, hearing Mr. Bernbach talk about communications and seeing Mr. Ogilvy communicate!"

Over at A&W Root Beer, where we had taken the brand from a test market to near national distribution, the MBA mentality had also taken a firm hold. When the brand became successful and profitable, Tom Fey, President of A&W, decided it was time we got some discipline. He hired a Marketing Director who had been trained at Procter & Gamble.

Mary Moore was smart enough to get off the account. My new A&W partner, Dick Gage, worked long and hard with me to make distinctive advertising within the constraints of P&G rules.

Sometimes we even succeeded. We have Andy Awards heads to prove it. But sometimes the successes were short-lived.

Here's the funniest (and saddest) thing that happened to us on the A&W account.

After much negotiating, the client had finally managed to get distribution in New York City, which, at last, made the brand truly national. We proposed that a special New York introductory campaign be created because the market was big enough to merit it and because New Yorkers were unlikely to get excited by the country-boys-and-girls stuff that had worked for us in other places. Tom Fey and Steve Stendstrom, his Marketing Director, bought the thinking, but they were a little scared of the sassy, very New Yorky campaign we came up with. We argued it back and forth, and suddenly there was no time to argue any more. Worse, from their point of view, there was no time to test before going on air, and they always tested. A&W management had no choice but to let us shoot our proposed campaign.

We did three spots, plus some radio that was a series of songs, not jingles; and when we presented to the bottlers, that hard-boiled bunch gave the advertising a roar of approval.

We went on air. At the same time, the spots were put into test by McCullom-Spielman, the client's usual testing service. It takes a couple of months to get final numbers in a McC-S test.

Before the numbers came in, A&W had established itself as the best-selling root beer in the New York Metro Market. More than that, it had actually expanded the root beer category. Success!

Then the test numbers came in. They proved that the campaign wouldn't work. When we pointed out that it *had* worked, the researchers said that was irrelevant. With the right advertising, A&W might have been even more successful.

So the campaign was pulled off the air.

MBAs do not deal in reality. I found out then, any more than they deal in fantasy.

Here is the saddest (and funniest) thing that happened to us on the A&W account.

When it came time to create a new national campaign, the client MBAs and those in the agency jointly decided that we must no longer sell the drink as root beer. We must sell it simply as a refreshing, mainstream soft drink. And we would do this by creating advertising that looked and sounded just like Coke's and Pepsi's.

Dick and I, with a lot of help from MacDougall, fought a vigorous and losing fight against this. So we went to work to be mainstream and distinctive at the same time.

When we thought we had it, we presented to Tom and Steve.

Tom, who hated the very idea of residuals for actors, always judged storyboards by first counting the number of bodies. These boards were crowded with them—dancing, being at a rock concert, playing volleyball, and romping at a beach party. Just like Coke and Pepsi.

We listened to his protests, explained that you couldn't do mainstream soft drink advertising with two or three kids in a spot, and asked him to judge the advertising, not the costs.

He tried. And he finally, reluctantly, said that he liked the campaign. But he was firm that he would never pay all those actors over and over again for one day of fun on the beach drinking free A&W. He asked us to consider shooting out of the country.

I agreed to have the spots bid with English companies and English actors, but even with that restriction I expressed my doubts about finding American-looking kids and locations.

The English prices, when they came in, had fairly high buy-out rates for the actors, who had to be members of Actors' Equity. Tom refused to consider it.

So we started getting bids from all over Europe, over loud protests from me. Nobody listened, even though our producer, Dick Perrott, and I were the only ones who had worked abroad. Hell, we had no MBAs, so who could take us seriously?

It got so bad that Sandy McGinnes, our Management Supervisor, started getting bids himself without working with Perrott. Dick had shot a lot of commercials abroad when he was at DDB and knew which houses to bid and which to avoid. So, naturally, Sandy beat him out by finding the lowest bid anywhere. It was from a Detroit company that nobody had ever heard of, and they proposed to shoot in Spain in coproduction with a Madrid firm nobody had ever heard of.

We were assured that it was easy to find Spanish kids who were indistinguishable from American kids. And for the beach party spot, we could recruit extras from all the British young people who crowd the Costa Blanca. Besides, we could do a lot of casting at the U.S. air base outside of Madrid, where there was a whole high school full of American kids.

I had trouble protesting, because I had never been in Spain.

So we went, including Ellen, Dick Gage's wife, and Dick Perrott's girl friend, for a month in sunny Spain. We had wanted to shoot in August but were assured we'd fry our brains, so we left in the first week of September.

It was freezing. There was snow in the hills just a few miles from Madrid. And that was just one of the little things that went wrong. The biggest problem was the casting, of course. The American kids at the air base all went rigid with fright when a camera was pointed at them. We had cast calls for three days up there and finally came away with just one nice, pretty girl, who was able to simulate being alive in front of a camera.

We went to the Costa Blanca, to a totally English resort town called Benidorm, to cast for the beach spot. The English kids were rough factory workers from Manchester, Leeds, and Liverpool. Most of the boys wore a gold earring in one ear, and all of them had tattoos on their forearms. We'd just have to shoot around it. Maybe makeup would help. There was nothing at all we could do about the girls, a hopelessly slutty-looking lot. All of them, boys and girls alike, were fish-belly white. More makeup, we said.

Casting wasn't our only problem. Wardrobe was a problem. Locations were a problem. Even props were a problem. But all the little problems paled in comparison to the big one, the one that nobody had foreseen.

None of the Spaniards or Brits in our cast had ever tasted root beer, and all of them found it disgusting. They could not bring the foamy mugs to their lips without grimacing in revulsion.

Root beer doesn't look like anything else, so there was no substitute we could use. We forced our amateur actors to drink our vile product. Some of them quit and forfeited the money rather than take another sip of the poison.

In the mandatory guzzling shots (right from the bottle, tilted high, shot against the sun) we found some of the braver boys who were willing to guzzle, but not to swallow. After each take, they spit out the stuff into a bucket while making noisy sounds of relief.

And, of course, when we printed the film, it was all there. We didn't have a single usable shot of a consumer enjoying consuming. Even when they weren't drinking, when they were just pulling bottles from an ice-filled cooler, you could see their distaste, their gorges rising in anticipation of the time when they would again be asked to drink.

An entire month's filming was wasted.

Naturally, the creative team got the blame.

The principal thing taught in the MBA schools is how to avoid ever getting the blame.

Then came the last day that I saw Bill Bernbach.

He had agreed to address the Boston Advertising Club, and because he was Bill Bernbach, the event was bigger than advertising; it was a public happening at which Governor Michael J. Dukakis and Mayor Kevin White were to be present, together with the principals and senior executives of every ad agency in town, accompanied by their most favored clients.

The Ad Club asked me, as the only DDB alumnus in Boston, to meet Bill at his hotel, take him to the hall, and see that he met all the right people during the pre-luncheon reception hour.

Bill seemed relieved and grateful to see me and allowed me to shepherd him about to meet the local dignitaries. First was Governor Dukakis, who remembered me and called me by my first name. Then it was Mayor White's turn. I had done some volunteer work for him, for the city actually, in the busing crisis. He, too, seemed pleased to see me and somewhat more pleased to be photographed with Bernbach.

The politicians dispensed with, the rest was an easy round with agency Presidents, Creative Directors, and some of the more prominent client folks, mostly my own.

Then it was time for lunch. I led Bill to the head table and left him to sit at HBM's table just below him.

Next to Bernbach was an empty seat; some dignitary had been unable to make it. He looked at the empty seat and then at me. He motioned me to come to talk to him.

"Come sit next to me," he said.

I told him that I didn't think it was a very good idea. Everyone at the head table had something to say, and I was not part of the program. I really belonged at my agency's table.

"No," he said. "I want you here. I need someone I know next to me."

I joined him reluctantly.

"Besides," he whispered to me as I sat down, "being seen with me might do you some good in this community."

MBAs were getting in everywhere. Even at Hood Dairies, one of our nicer clients, a Brand System was installed, and each of the boxes on the chart was filled with an ex-Procter Brand Manager.

An aside: I have since learned that "ex-Procter" is not a high recommendation. P&G management does not let its winners get away if they can help it. The people who leave Procter at the Brand Manager level are usually the ones who have had it made clear that they had little chance of advancement.

I didn't work on Hood, so I have this story second-hand, but I can't resist telling it.

The client had requested a spot for Milk. The creative team, Dana Jones and Bill Boch, faced up to the problem of selling a branded commodity in an interesting manner.

They came up with a talking head, a stand-up announcer, but in this case, the announcer was to be a talking cow. Not an animated cartoon, but a real cow with its lips moving in synch with a voice track. They had written a smart, funny script for the cow and went happily off to present it.

Late in the day, Dana dropped into my office and sat down, looking a little dazed. "You won't believe this," he said, "but I swear it's true."

They had presented the talking cow to the Assistant Brand Manager, the Brand Manager, and the Marketing Director, all of whom made careful notes. Then, in the approved P&G manner, the Marketing Director asked the Assistant Brand Manager for his thoughts.

The assistant looked at his notes and then asked Dana if, in the creative development process, he had considered any other animals.

It had finally happened, completely. Boston had caught up with New York, where the MBAs had been running the show for nearly a decade.

It wasn't fun any more, and for me that meant that I had best be moving on. Besides, I had been away from New York for ten years, and I was beginning to miss it. I tried to talk HBM into starting a New York office (we already had our Broadcast Production office there, and it would have been easy to build on that) but the management felt that, while they did want to do it, this wasn't the time.

There was nothing to hold me in Boston, other than a great fondness for the city and the friends I had made there in the last six years. But as for work, I could see no account in the house that I wanted to work on. Parker Brothers had become a miserable piece of business where the white bread clients made all the white bread choices and where it was forbidden (literally) to cast a kid who wasn't blond or red-headed with freckles. Fantasy was out. Fun was out. The work the agency was forced to do was largely dreary and logical.

The Spanish mess had resulted in A&W requesting a new team, so I couldn't work on that. And the few other good accounts in the agency had fine people tending to them, turning out first-class work.

So I went to New York.

Only a few months later, Mal MacDougall also quit to come to New York. Humphrey and Browning had decided to make Ed Eskandarian, Mal's counterpart on the Account Management side, President of HBM. The job should have gone to MacDougall because it was he and his creative vision and leadership that had built the agency from its $5 million beginning to some $50 million and a national creative reputation in less than a decade. But it was decided that Mal was not *serious* enough to be a President. He got excited. He laughed too loud and hard. He gave stern lectures on advertising to dull clients who wanted boring work. He had no patience for fools and ordered them out of his office. As the fools, by then, outnumbered the clever, Humphrey and Browning decided that MacDougall could not ever be a President.

Mal went to SSC&B as Executive Creative Director of the Whole Damn World, or words to that effect. In a year's time they made him President.

I went to work for my old friends from early DDB days, Ron Rosenfeld and Len Sirowitz.

The Time Machine was put in mothballs.

Bob Levenson told me a great story I had never heard before, though it must have been kicking around for about a hundred years.

It was about J. Walter Thompson, the man, not the agency.

Mr. Thompson, after working very late one night, was going home on the El, the elevated railway that preceded the subway, pleased to be alone in the car. At the first stop, however, an old and slightly drunk "sandwich man" boarded, his billboards hanging fore and aft from his shoulders.

He wanted to talk to Thompson. Thompson didn't want to, but was polite about it.

The sandwich man asked Thompson what he did for a living, and Thompson told him he was in advertising.

The old guy gave him a sympathetic look, patted him on the shoulder, and said sadly, "Oh, yes. Ain't it hell when the wind blows?"

AIN'T IT HELL?

One Sunday at home, I got a phone call from Paris, from a man with an Irish brogue who said his name was Padraig O'Curry and that he was a management consultant specializing in executive recruitment.

"A head hunter," I said.

"I suppose you could call it that," he said in a regretful tone. "Point is," he went on, "would you be interested in a very senior position in Europe?"

I told him that I would not, but how nice of him to ask.

"I won't take no for an answer until you've heard the thing out," O'Curry said. "I'll be in New York in a week, so you can let me give you lunch and hear what I have to say. What could be fairer than that?"

We set a date, and when I had hung up I told Ellen about the call. "No," she said firmly. "I hated being uprooted from Westport to go to Boston. I worked hard to put down new roots, and when they were finally established, we uprooted again to come back to Westport. We're home now, and I am not going back to Europe."

"I told him I wouldn't be interested in going back," I protested.

"Then why are you having lunch with him?"

I told her that I liked his manner and his accent and that I always liked a free lunch. Besides, I was curious to find out how he had got to me; I'd probably learn that we had European friends in common.

On the day of the lunch Ellen said, "I hope you enjoy your

meeting, but tonight I don't want to hear one word about what a great job it is that you're going to refuse on my account."

I told her that I wanted roots as much as she did, that I knew we couldn't root in Europe, that it was a finished phase of our lives, that I was done with Gypsying, that I had finally grown up, and a lot of other things.

She remained looking dubious as I waved goodbye.

Padraig O'Curry was a slim, rumpled man with a pleasant face. He appeared to be in his late thirties. Over a drink he told me how he had gotten to me. We had at least half a dozen friends in common in France, Germany, and England. His closest friend was Uli Wiesendanger, who was the W in TBWA and who had worked for me years before in Germany where we had also become good friends.

J. Walter Thompson was looking for someone to be titled Executive Creative Director, Europe, but whose real job was to bring order out of the chaos that was Ford of Europe. The search for this person had been going on for nearly two years, which was not surprising given the specifications.

The first requirement alone made the job almost impossible to fill: a previous history of having worked successfully as an agency's Creative Director in Europe. It was hard to imagine anyone who had done that who would want to do it again.

To add to Padraig's search problem, the candidate must have a solid automotive background, must have a strong creative reputation both in the United States and Europe, and must be willing to live in Germany. Fluency in German would be nice, too, as well as functional ability in a couple of other languages.

I told Padraig that I knew only five people who could match those specs, that two of them were partners in agencies of their own, two were permanent fixtures in agencies where they had top management jobs, and the fifth was me. I added that I was sure he knew and had already talked to the other four.

He laughed, and we showed our hands, so to speak, by writing the names on napkins and comparing the short lists. They were not only identical, but we had written them in the same order.

After we had eaten and swapped gossip about friends and

acquaintances, Padraig gave me a folder to examine. It was Thompson's job order to Padraig's firm, John Stork & Partners, plus an outline of the Executive Creative Director's responsibilities. As I skimmed through it, he said, "If you want the job, I should think you'd have no difficulty making a very profitable arrangement. I wouldn't say you have them over a barrel, mind, but all the same . . . ."

I told him that I just didn't want the job.

He mentioned a salary that made me dizzy, but I held firm. "It's not a question of money," I said.

That night I did tell Ellen about the offer, but not that I thought it was a wonderful job. It didn't sound wonderful, only rich.

She looked relieved and happy.

I saw Padraig once more before he returned to Paris. We had drinks and a pleasant chat while I told him that I was determined not to take the job, and that I'd do some thinking and sniffing about for him to see if I could help by putting him on to a good potential candidate.

I put J. Walter Thompson and Europe out of my mind.

About a month later, I got a call from a man at Thompson who said his name was Ross (I've forgotten his first name) and that he was in charge of JWT International. He asked if I would be willing to take the time to come see him and talk a bit about the job.

I am always willing to talk to anyone about anything, so I made a date, but I warned him first that I had no interest in going to work for him.

Ross, like all senior Thompson executives, was pleasant, intelligent, articulate, and persuasive. He talked about the challenge offered by the job and the rewards to be won by merely accepting the challenge. If I were actually to succeed, why there was no telling what . . . .

Among the rewards suitable for a man in my position (aged fifty-three, no children at home or in college, free to live as and where my wife and I chose) was the pleasure of a constant European vacation, almost. I would be traveling often to one or another JWT office: Paris, London, Madrid, Vienna, Stockholm, Milan, and many more. Of course Ellen would go along when she chose—all expenses paid, first class, naturally.

"Though, with the amount you'll be earning, that will hardly be a consideration." He named a figure 20 percent higher than the one Padraig had suggested, and Padraig's had made my head spin.

He then went on to speak of six weeks' vacation a year, an annual home leave, the pleasures of living in Frankfurt.

I stopped him. "Have you ever lived in Germany?" I asked.

He hadn't, but he'd traveled a lot there with his German-born wife. They had honeymooned along the Romantische Strasse, the lovely Romantic Road through the Black Forest and the enchanted villages of Baden.

As it turned out, he had never lived abroad at all and had only very recently been put in charge of International. His career had been in Chicago.

I could see there wasn't going to be a whole lot he could tell me. In fact, he had already told me everything he had wanted to when he casually mentioned the salary.

I thanked him for his interest in me, but said that I was not his man. I had had Europe, and this could only be a step backwards.

"You don't mind if I call you again?" he asked. "There are a few people here who would like to meet you. Maybe after talking to them you might change your mind."

I told him I was always willing to talk.

During the next month or so I met Jack Peters, who was top account man on Ford and who outlined the problems JWT had been having with Ford of Europe (which was usually referred to as Foe for its initials). Peters seemed to know a lot about cars and a little, only a little, about advertising. His main thrust seemed to be to determine whether I was a Car Man. When he became reasonably sure that I was (I was not, but I acted like one), he did a nice job of welcoming me aboard. He paid no attention to my protests that I had not accepted the job and had no intention of doing so.

I saw Ross right after meeting Peters. "He's already called me. He thinks you're worth a lot more than we've offered and I agreed." I braced myself for a shock, and I got one.

I told him that I'd discuss it with Ellen.

Money had suddenly become a serious problem for us. We had left Boston without having sold our house and were renting in Westport. We had been sure, when we left Boston in spring-time, that our historic colonial home with its fine view of Hingham Harbor would sell in a matter of weeks. Now it was late fall, and we had no offers worth considering.

The problem was the outrageous price of oil in 1980 and the fact that the big, rambling house with its twelve rooms and five fireplaces took a minimum of 3,000 gallons of fuel a year to keep comfortably chilly in the New England style. It seemed unlikely that it would sell before spring and meanwhile was costing us a lot of money each month.

Ross had asked, during our first talk, if we owned a home. When I told him our situation, he had suggested that it was not unlikely that Thompson would buy the house, or at least assume its costs until it was sold for an agreed price. If they had to sell it for less, they would make up the difference.

Since that first talk, this offer had assumed some real importance. The house deal plus the doubly raised salary would get us out of trouble.

Ellen recognized the sense of it and reluctantly said that if it meant getting our economic act together, she'd put up with another tour of duty in Europe. After all, we had had a lot of fun the first time; we did have a lot of friends there, favorite cousins in Paris, places we loved to visit, places we had never been, and so on.

Before the evening was over, we were happily fantasizing about our new adventure.

After years of looking to fill the job, everything was suddenly in a rush. I was asked to fly to Frankfurt to meet George

Black, head of the office there, where I would be headquartered. From Frankfurt I was to go to Paris to have dinner with Jack Cronin, President of J. Walter Thompson, Europe (an organization I was later to learn did not, in fact, exist).

The weekend they had asked me to come was Thanksgiving, and I at first refused. Unfortunately, it was the only date that both Black and Cronin would be available until after the first of the year. Reluctantly, I went, summoning again Ellen's bad feelings about the whole venture.

Frankfurt was drizzly and chill. The smell of soft coal still hung over Germany, though less than in the 60s. The city's outskirts were bleak with ugly new housing projects. I could not believe that I was willing to live here again, just for money.

George Black made me feel better about the place. A bearded giant, he was entirely unthreatening. On the contrary, his welcome was warm and genial. We talked about life in the new Germany, about music, literature, art, food, and wine. George said he hoped I would take the job, if only because he needed a playmate. He had been living in Germany for twenty years, most of them without steady American companionship.

A wonderful dinner at a charming little French restaurant with George and his wife Bibi followed by a brief tour of the West End, a lovely district near the office, where we would probably want to live, made me feel much better about the prospect of a few years in Frankfurt.

George suggested that if I was still unsure after this visit and my meeting the next day in Paris, I ought to come back for a few days after the first of the year and bring Ellen with me. Perhaps a visit with the Blacks might give her some enthusiasm for living here.

I thought it a fine idea, and we parted with seasonal good wishes and anticipation of a visit in January.

Our January visit was a great success. We traveled first class, as I had done on my previous visit, were housed in a spacious suite in the Frankfurter Hof, a grand old landmark, and were greeted with pleasure by the Blacks.

The first night they gave us dinner at their home in a village in the nearby Taunus Mountains. The second night, Ellen and I took the senior JWT staff on Ford business to dinner, and their reactions to us were somewhere between courteous and suspicious—just the right tone for Germans.

The next day we flew to Paris for dinner with my cousins and told them that we had decided to live in Germany again and would once more be near-neighbors.

When we got home, I called our eldest daughter at her home in Vermont to tell her the news. "Oh, Dad," she said impatiently, "when are you going to grow up?"

The next day in New York, I met with Ross to tell him that I would take the job. Delighted, he asked Ellen and me to join him and his wife for dinner to celebrate.

We ate at a chic, expensive restaurant and drank superb German wines while we talked about the pleasures of the Romantische Strasse. Toward the end of the evening, Ross told me that I would find both JWT Europe and Ford of Europe to be very peculiar and political organizations and should I run into any problems that I couldn't handle myself, I was to call him without hesitation.

"I will be your rabbi," he said. "Everyone should have a rabbi."

I joined JWT on February 1 to spend three months in the New York office getting background on Ford and learning what I could about how things were done at Thompson.

I flew to Palm Springs for a few days to join the JWT German creative team on Ford, who were there doing their annual shoot of TV spots, catalog stills, and ads. I asked why they were shooting European cars, quite different from U.S. Fords, in the American desert. What was wrong with European backgrounds, where the cars would be sold and used?

"Europe looks so old-fashioned," I was told.

I met some of my German clients, who were quite happily at home in Palm Springs and clearly would not have welcomed any suggestion that this year the shoot be in Mannheim or Mainz.

I also met my partner-to-be, Ole Kirk-Jensen, who had just joined Thompson to be Management Supervisor, Europe on the Ford business. It had taken Padraig as long to fill that job as mine, and Kirk told me that it had taken a lot of persuasion to make him accept. He had been with Renault for many years, the last five or six as Advertising Director, living in Paris. He loved Paris, he told me sadly, and knew it would be difficult for him and his family to adjust to living in London.

"London?" I said. "If we're partners, why are you going to live in London while I'm going to live in Frankfurt?"

"Frankfurt? That's crazy," Kirk said. "The client is in England."

"But the Ford of Europe creative department is in Frankfurt," I told him. "A bunch of expatriate Brits and an American who once owned an agency in England, somewhere in Yorkshire."

Kirk said that they could be wherever they wanted to be, but that I had to be in London to work with him. If he could make it happen I would love it, I told him. Ellen would, too, as she had always wanted to live in London after the taste of it we had during DDB days.

In the months that followed, a great deal of effort on Kirk's part and on mine went into getting all of us in one office, preferably in England where the client was. We never even got to first base.

I spent my first three months in Frankfurt getting to know the cars and and the markets, visiting the Ford offices in England on a nearly weekly basis, and finding out that Ross had been talking through his hat.

I was not allowed to travel first class. I was not allowed to take Ellen with me at agency expense. There were no trips to Paris, Vienna, Milan, Madrid. I was told to concentrate first on Ford of Germany (Fog) and only later on Foe. These orders from George Black conflicted strangely with the visits to England, where nobody wanted to talk about the German market.

In September, after we had seen Ford's presentation of the

new line of cars, it was time to go to work. I tried to coordinate the efforts of the German Group with the European Group, but nobody paid any attention to what I said.

I talked it over with George and told him that if those turkeys didn't follow orders I would have to hire people who would. He could figure out what to do with my rejects.

George opened a locked drawer and took out a large sheet of paper. "I guess I've never shown you this," he said, handing it to me.

It was an organization chart showing a complex array of boxes and reporting lines. Up at the very top was my name in a large box. There were no lines connected to the box.

"You mean that no one reports to me?" I asked incredulously. "And I report to no one?"

"Technically yes," George said.

"But actually?"

"Also yes," he said.

I asked for a copy of the chart, but was told that it was confidential. He locked it up again and I left, not knowing what to do next.

Of course I knew what to do next. I called Ross, my rabbi in New York.

But Ross was no longer in charge of International. He had been returned to Chicago.

For the next three months I watched the Fog group create six campaigns, each exquisitely and expensively rendered and none having a central selling concept or theme. Down the hall the Foe group was busy creating a mere three or four campaigns, as elaboraterly rendered as Fog's.

I commented, protested, enjoined, and finally gave up. I filled my time instead by writing a stream of memos to George and to Jack Cronin suggesting new and better ways to organize and to create meaningful work. None was answered, as I anticipated.

I accompanied the Fog group to watch their presentation, and it became clear to me why so much had been spent on beautiful renderings. The clients never commented on ideas, but talked a lot about the illustrations, which would never be used in advertising and only served to show what the photography would be like. More or less.

"I think it needs a higher angle," said one.

"But then you wouldn't get that beautiful highlight on the front fender," said another.

"I like that ad," said the head man, "but this one is terrible. This car should never be shown in white, and it looks like hell without the optional wheel covers."

They talked like that all morning. Nobody ever mentioned a headline or a selling theme. And they thought they were talking about advertising.

Before it was time for the Foe presentation, I had another discussion with George. I told him that I could see now why everybody wanted to keep me out of the picture. Simply, everybody was perfectly happy with things as they were.

I asked him what had ever made JWT think they needed an Executive Creative Director Europe.

A former head of Ford of Europe had given the order, as George told me, to a former Thompson top exec. The search was started, and when it was done, two years later, the problem had disappeared, together with the two executives. But no one had the authority to override the original order.

I know that sounds unreal, but that's more or less how it was explained to me.

"So Kirk and I are cures for which there is no known disease?"

"Exactly," George said with his usual twinkle.

George had a solution to my problem. "It's all a question of positioning. I'll reposition you as a sort of in-house creative consultant, not only on Ford but everything. I'll say that any Creative Director who is in doubt about a campaign or an ad or commercial can talk to you."

Did you ever meet a Creative Director who admitted to being in doubt about anything?

The day the repositioning memo came out was the day that everyone stopped talking to me, for fear of appearing to be in doubt.

Except for the days that Kirk was in town, I never again had lunch with anyone from Thompson.

Ellen and I went home for a month's visit in December and decided in a matter of days that we didn't want to go back to Germany with Thompson. We started looking for a house.

We returned to Germany on January 2, and on the 3rd I told George that I believed JWT to be in clear violation of contract and asked him what the company would do about it.

It only took three days for him to come back with a satisfactory proposition.

A month later, after only nine months in Germany, the company shipped us home (my only first class flight since arriving with Ellen) together with our household goods: furniture, rugs, books, records, paintings, and objects.

I didn't know what I was coming home to, but I knew what I wasn't going to do. I wasn't going to work for an ad agency if I could help it.

INTERLUDE, WITH MBAs

Ad agencies weren't my problem, of course, and I wasn't trying to kid myself that they were. My most recent problem, the adventure with JWT, was an inevitable result of taking a job I didn't want, a job that never made any sense, just because it paid a lot of money.

I had always believed, with George Lois, that if advertising isn't any fun, there is no point in doing it.

But a quest for fun hadn't done me a whole lot of good either, had it? HBM and the Boston days had been plenty of fun, but the sadness of the last year there had equaled the joys of the first five.

McCaffery & McCall and the tour of the world had been fun, but it ended in a sour reality.

I recognized that my present problems, as much as my past pleasures, were simply a matter of timing. What I really wanted, I could never have again: a job in a good agency in the 60s.

So, in February of 1982, I went to work for Weston Group, the marketing company headed by my old friend Jack Lewis, from which I had rented a room and office services nearly a decade ago after leaving my agency.

Weston Group had long since outgrown the cottage next door to what had once been my Greek Revival mansion. Now they were in handsome modern quarters in an office building on the bank of the Saugatuck River. In addition to the three principals, there were six or seven consultants, mostly MBAs and all either ex-Procter or ex-General Foods.

I had free-lanced with the Group ever since first meeting

them, including the time we were in Germany, where I helped by developing contacts for them and opening doors for their new business pitches. It was easy to fit in full-time.

The main business of Weston Group was new product development, for which a Creative Director is needed. You see, new products are never actually developed until it can be proved that there is a market for them. Doing this involves creating product ideas, expressing them in the form of concept ads, and exposing these ads to focus groups.

Based on focus group learning, ads are refined or scrapped, new ideas developed, old ideas altered. Then back to do more focus groups.

If this sounds logical to you, you have already been brainwashed by MBAs.

During my first year and a half at Weston Group we exposed countless concept ads to countless consumers on behalf of a major distiller. We were trying to develop a new aperitif that would be a substitute for the unbranded "glass of white wine" that Americans were then ordering at bars and restaurants and guzzling at a mad rate.

All ideas foundered on the recurrent questions, "But what does it taste like? Why can't we try some?" They couldn't try some because it didn't exist, and it would never exist unless lots of consumers swore they had to have some.

The concept of wine coolers was often exposed to these groups and always rejected out of hand. "Fruit juice and wine? Ugh."

Then the California Cooler happened. Just happened.

Two guys from California, Michael Crete and Stuart Bewley, decided to take a chance on bottling their home recipe of fruit juices and white wine. Their lack of experience and knowledge stood in the way of nothing except consumer research.

They went blithely and blindly into the market and created a whole new category with a dozen or so competing brands. Coolers became the second largest selling wine type in only five years. Seventy million cases went down the American gullet, and $1.4 billion in sales crossed retailers' counters.

The founders sold California Cooler and became instant millionaires.

But I've got the data to prove to you that wine coolers are a lousy idea.

It wasn't all wine coolers and roses at Weston Group. We worked on imported German beer, pasta, snack crackers, brandy, plastic wrap, and even duller things. I didn't mind at all. It was even fun, traveling to Los Angeles or Philadelphia to sit in a dim room behind a one-way glass and watch consumers tear my concept ads apart.

"That ad insults my intelligence!"

"That ad is offensive to women!"

"I would never buy that; the package doesn't look biodegradable!"

"That advertising is trying to put something over on us. I don't know what, but I know it is!"

Sometimes one or another of them said something worth hearing and remembering, like the woman in a group discussing probable trends for the 80s. "I don't think I'm going to like the 80s. The 80s won't be about anything except computers and being thin."

There was some personal development going on for me too. I learned to speak Marketing, to understand the peculiar jargon spoken (and, sadly, written) by the consultants and our clients. Packaged-Goods-Speak would come in handy some day, I knew, even if only to be able to converse with the stranger next to me on a long flight.

The work was easy. I could write a dozen concept statements before lunch, come back to discuss the "ads" with the art director, and still be on the golf course by three to play nine holes.

If you don't know what a concept ad is, you've led a very sheltered life in advertsing. If you want to know, here's a brief description that will help explain the quotation marks around the word *"ads"* a few lines back.

A concept ad mustn't look like advertising. It must present a selling proposition in a few simple words with a minimum of graphics. Let's say we're trying to create a position for a new entry in the detergent market. The product doesn't exist; the concept ads will help determine what it should be. All of the "ads" show nothing but a box of detergent. One "ad" is headlined, "You can't buy a cheaper detergent." Another says, "Gets colors brighter while it gets whites whiter." Another, "Kills germs while it cleans." Still another claims, "Makes your laundry smell as clean as air-dried." Another claims, "Concentrated strength so you use less." And so on and so on.

These are used as what's called "consumer stimuli" to get laundrophile ladies talking in focus groups.

Creating this sort of thing is essentially mindless work, but in many ways it beat working in what big advertising agencies had become.

I had no thought of going back until one day when I got a phone call that made me react like a dalmatian hound to the sound of the firehouse alarm.

ON THE ROAD AGAIN

"We're wondering whether you'd be interested in joining us as International Creative Director, to make some sense of our foreign offices."

It was Bob Curry in Boston, calling from Hill Holliday Connors Cosmopulos.

I told him I'd sure be interested in talking about it, and that I had a few questions we could handle right then on the phone. Unfortunately, Bob didn't know a thing. He had been picked to make the call because he and I were friends back in the days when we both worked at Humphrey Browning MacDougall.

"You'll really have to talk to Jay Hill," Bob said. "I'll tell him you're interested, and he'll get in touch."

Hill called me about ten minutes later, and we made a date for me to come to Boston the following week.

I was given a warm welcome and an immediate job offer. Jay wanted me to solve some tough problems, including finding top-notch Creative Directors for key offices such as London. This was not going to be easy, I pointed out, since HHCC insisted on creating all work for Wang, their only international client and the biggest client in all foreign offices, right at home in Boston.

"That's not going to interest top creative talent," I said, "and I gather that you're not willing to give any part of the operations away, either."

Jay admitted that was true.

"So how do I attract good people?"

"If we knew the answer to that we wouldn't need you."

That wasn't the only problem that came with the job. It was

also obvious that with only five foreign offices, the job could not take my full time. I would not be able to do it operating out of their embryo New York office, where there was no work for me to do, but would have to move back to Boston so that I could work on agency creative projects between trips abroad. I didn't mind, but I didn't think Ellen would take kindly to it, having rerooted happily in Connecticut in a house we both loved.

The inducements were strong, however. Jay agreed that if I were to take the job, the agency would pay for Ellen's travel with me whenever she wanted to join me. First class, of course. The salary offer was very handsome. And the perks included a company car of my choice, club dues for a country club, town clubs in Boston and New York, plus the club in London where I had been a member for more than twenty years.

There was also the sense that HHCC was on the brink of a new phase in its corporate life; that it had outgrown the puns and silliness of earlier years and could possibly emerge as an exciting new creative presence. It was a powerful temptation to be a part of it.

Ellen had spent the day with friends in Boston. As we drove home, we discussed the possibilities of the job and the problem of the return to Massachusetts. She surprised me by saying that she didn't mind at all, that she was equally at home in both places, and that in any case, she felt I ought to get out of the silly work I had been doing for the last year and a half.

We agreed to give the thing a week without serious thought about it, just to let the idea hang around and see if we became excited by it or not.

That was on Monday. By Tuesday I could think of nothing else. I could not imagine turning down the job.

On Wednesday, I had a lunch date with Bob Levenson, a thing we tried to do from time to time, usually at intervals of about a year. Bob was Vice Chairman Creative at DDB International, and it would be a good opportunity to ask his thoughts about the HHCC job and how on earth I was going to find smart Creative Directors for them.

We met at DDB's offices, and as we went out, he asked if lunch at the Four Seasons was okay with me. "On DDB, of course," he added.

It was the first suspicion I had that he had asked me to lunch not just to swap yarns but to offer me a job.

Bob didn't waste any time. The job offer came with the drink, and I accepted before we had taken a sip.

Somebody up there liked me, it seemed. But he liked me better when I was out in the world doing things than when I was vegetating among the MBAs and playing bad golf in the dull and lazy afternoons.

I returned to Doyle Dane Bernbach in June of 1983, after an absence of fifteen years. It seemed less like a homecoming than a haunting, in which I was the ghost. Or like a visit to a once fashionable resort out of season: Deauville in November, the pale yellow sun on the bleached boardwalk serving only to recall the warmth of summers past, the laughter of children long grown old.

The hallways were quiet. Most doors were closed. There were no ads on display in the public areas, except on a long wall behind a row of secretaries on the executive floor. These ads were, for the most part, not very exciting. The aim seemed to be for competence, professionalism, a certain new slickness. I saw nothing to shake me up and make me think, except the fact that there was nothing to shake me up and make me think.

Bill Bernbach had been dead for a year, and his agency was only a little behind him. As one ghost to another, I saluted his portrait and drifted on, like ectoplasm, in my melancholy tour.

My ghostly status was quite real. I wasn't actually part of the place, but was only quartered there. My work would be in foreign lands.

I cruised around the creative hallways and, where there was a familiar name on the door, stuck my head in to say hello. A few of the old faces were still there: Les Feldman, Helmut Krone, Charlie Picarillo (like me, a late returnee), Judy Protas, Dave Reider, Bill Taubin; Bob Gage and Jack Dillon were still working together, but seldom came in to the office. Ever since Jack's stroke, they worked a few days a week at Gage's home in Pound Ridge. Their few appearances seemed as spectral as mine.

Counting Bob Levenson and me, there were only ten of us, of the thirty-three who were at DDB when I first arrived.

I went to lunch with Helmut.

I said that I hoped he would consider working with me in International. We had made a good team in the past and maybe, without the restrictions of uptight American clients, we could do something good again.

"You wouldn't want to work with me now," he said. "I'm not interested in ideas any more. I don't care about headlines or copy. Concepts are out. Execution is all that matters these days."

"That can't be true," I began, but Helmut cut me off.

"I don't want to talk about it; just face up to the fact. The public doesn't want ideas. They certainly don't want words. They just want a new look. I don't want to discuss advertising. Let's find a new subject."

"But what you said is worth discussing," I said.

"You're all business, aren't you?" he said sharply. "Don't you have some other life left?"

I laughed and told him that I had almost forgotten how much I liked him.

"That's funny," he said solemnly. "I didn't forget how much I like you."

Bob said we would have to hire an art director for me to work with because everyone on staff considered a job in International to be a terminal disease. He asked me to make up a short list of candidates.

My list couldn't have been shorter. It consisted of one name, Don Blauweiss. Don was at Benton & Bowles, where he had been for the last ten years. For two of those years, when I was with JWT, Don was Creative Director of B&B in Brussels. We had had drinks in Frankfurt and a happy renewal of our old acquaintance that had begun in 1956 when he worked for DDB's Sales Promotion Department. He had also worked for DDB in Düsseldorf, a few years after I had left. Later he had worked at Ogilvy (again, after I was gone) on Mercedes and had done a lot of production abroad.

It was a perfect match, I thought. Don knew how to work in foreign languages and cultures. He was fluent in German, Spanish, and Portuguese, and could get by pretty well in French and Flemish. He was also a first-class art director.

I took him to lunch and put the proposition to him. He was interested, but needed some time. His ten-year profit-sharing plan would mature in the fall, and it would cost him a lot to leave now. Could I wait?

I talked it over with Bob, and he in turn talked to Don. It was agreed that we would wait for him and that meanwhile we would borrow an art director for three months.

Bob suggested Charlie Abrams. I had never heard of him, but Bob said he had teamed very well with him himself, on Polaroid and on Procter & Gamble. That was good enough for me. Roy Grace, who was Chairman and Creative Director of DDB, agreed to lend us Charlie for three months. We worried a bit about taking him because Roy's enmity for Bob Levenson was irrationally acute, and we feared that Charlie might be viewed as tainted meat after association with us. It could possibly lose him the chance of returning to Roy's department. Charlie said that he was aware of that, and still wanted to take his chances with us. I liked his guts and looked forward to working with him.

Charlie looked like a kid to me. He was thirty-six and looked ten years younger than that. I was fifty-six and don't care to know how old I may have appeared. It did not look like a promising partnership, but personal chemistry works in strange ways. We hit it off immediately and started turning out exciting work as easily as if we had been teamed for years.

We worked on Atari, creating and producing pattern advertising that could be effective in all of Europe, overcoming differences in language, culture, and the state of market development in video games.

We also worked on Chivas Regal International, which had asked us for a series of magazine ads. We did a dozen, all fated never to run, including one ad that we will always think the best Chivas ad either of us had ever done. It was a bottle with a gift tag reading, "You're fired." The headline was "There's a nice way to say almost anything."

Don joined us in the fall, in time to start with me on a new campaign for Polaroid International. There was enough work to

keep both Don and Charlie busy, and Charlie elected to stay
with us, knowing that the decision would prevent him from ever
going back to work for Roy.

Charlie and I flew to Paris and to Hamburg and commuted
to San Francisco for Atari. All of us flew with our wives to ac-
company Bob in creative staff meetings in London, Düsseldorf,
Brussels, and Paris. Somehow I was able to keep up with both
accounts and both partners, so I turned down the idea of hiring
another writer.

This kind of busy-ness just didn't seem like work.

Our problems began with Atari.

The clients at this Silicon Valley maker of the electronic
Hula Hoop, the microchip Nehru jacket, were obsessed with being leading-edge, state-of-the-art, with-it, hip, au courant, and
as young as they could pretend to get away with.

One look at me was all it took to convince them I would
never understand and be able to write for their teenaged target
market. Charlie passed muster, all right, but I was clearly hopeless.

They hated that they liked our work, but put up with it for
the first round of spots for the big fall season. They almost liked
the fact, I think, that sales responded poorly. They could blame
the advertising, call for a young, new creative team, and move
on into the glowing future of an ever-expanding market.

Bob teamed Charlie up with a smart young writer, Jeff Lin-
der, who looked almost young enough to be Charlie's son. Don
and I were asked to create a second campaign. I didn't like being
in competition with one of my partners, but Atari had been
promised at least two campaigns to review.

Charlie and Jeff did a very contemporary, very teen, very
good-looking campaign. Don and I did something else. We presented, in turn, in a huge conference room packed with people.
The distress of the Atari people was palpable when they decided
to go with the campaign the two old guys had come up with.
They thought they would be stuck with us forever.

What they hadn't noticed was that there was not going to be

any forever for them. While we were talking advertising, the video game business all but disappeared. Atari stopped advertising, leaving our International Division with only one real client, Polaroid.

Don and I were busy creating campaigns, one after the other, for Polaroid International, trying to understand the mindset of their new marketing director who had no background in the camera business. He was the predictable MBA with packaged-goods experience who was seriously out of his depth marketing a device that could not be viewed as "a box of product." It was okay with us, we knew the game, and we had the necessary patience.

And then we were blind-sided. While we had our eyes on the marketing guy, Polaroid realigned its management and put International in the hands of a man whose experience was in domestic sales. He took a trip, met the Managing Directors of the foreign subsidiaries, and heard each one ask for control of his own advertising.

Now this is the commonest complaint in the world of international marketing. Each national believes his country to be unique. Maybe made-in-America pattern advertising is just fine for most of the world, but here in Ratagonia there is a taboo against showing a woman's elbow. Elsewhere it is shocking bad manners to ask for the order. In another land, competitiveness is out, while in the neighboring country, one is told, the product must be compared factually to its competitor because the consumer craves only information.

Of course, Bob and Don and I knew about this. Most of it was garbage and simply untrue. What it really reflected was each Polaroid chief's belief that he was an advertising authority and his dislike of taking orders. Simply, it was the classic not-invented-here factor.

Polaroid's newly appointed International Maven thought he had discovered in this old and widespread condition the reason for Polaroid's sagging sales abroad. In a burst of undeserved self-confidence he turned all the foreign subsidiaries loose to create their own campaigns. Their local DDB agencies were all too eager to comply, having long resented being handed advertising to translate and run.

Overnight, our little group had lost our other client, without the agency having actually lost a thing.

The problem was entirely ours: Bob's, Don's, Charlie's, and mine. We would have to find some new ways to justify our existence.

When in doubt, get out of town.

We all packed up and went to Europe for another series of visitations and a two-day meeting with European Creative Directors and some of their Managing Directors. One of the subjects was our availability (desperate need, in fact) to help them with creative projects such as new business pitches, especially for locally generated campaigns with multinational needs.

They heard us out with not much enthusiasm from the creatives, but with some signs of real interest from their counterparts in Account Management.

Work began coming in. First I was asked to attend a few days of meetings in Switzerland in which an attempt would be made to create a compelling new positioning that would save a maker of expensive Swiss watches from going down the tube with the rest of the Swiss watch makers. Ellen and I took the opportunity to have a few days' vacation in London first.

Within minutes of my arrival in the DDB office there, I was asked by Nikolai Von Dellingshausen, who was in charge of DDB Europe, if I could spare a couple of days to go to Madrid. The office there was pitching the Spanish Ministry of Tourism for a campaign that would run in English language publications throughout Europe. They needed an English or American writer to assist them.

I had four days before needing to be in Switzerland, so I agreed. Ellen and I flew to Madrid the next day.

The Spanish staff welcomed me warmly, assured me that they had a great campaign concept and good English copy, but they knew they needed someone to check it out.

I checked it out. It was horrible.

The campaign theme was all wrong, and the language was a weird, homemade kind of Esperanto English. I explained this to Paco Torres, head of the DDB office, with the help of a translator. He had trouble accepting what I said but finally went with me as an act of faith. I explained that the theme (I've since forgotten what it was) would be interesting to and understood by Spaniards only and second, that his slogan (also forgotten now) would make no sense whatever in the two languages I knew best, English and German. He agreed to let me make a new campaign.

I called Don and told him the story. He said he'd get on a plane to Madrid that night.

We worked for one day. At the end of it we had a slogan that was so perfect, so simple, so obvious that we couldn't believe it hadn't been used before by some southern country.

It was "Spain. Everything under the Sun."

I called Bob in New York and tried it on him. He liked it as much as we did, and had the same doubts about its availability. He said he'd get Legal to check it out and get back to us as soon as possible.

I flew to Zurich, leaving Don to start putting ads together. Ellen flew home.

The three days in the remote town high in French Switzerland were pleasant and meaningless. We did what we had set out to do, which was to create a positioning statement that was pure bafflegab. The Japanese watchmakers who had without doubt planted spies and placed bugs at our secretive meeting could all relax; their business was in no danger from the Swiss.

Back in Madrid, I learned that our slogan was available. Don and I put together a magazine campaign of at least a dozen ads designed to convince upscale Europeans that Spain offered more than cheap beach vacation packages, which was all that the Tourist Ministry had been selling for the past two decades.

A month later a Telex arrived in New York to tell us that we had won the business, had to create a lot of new ads, and to please come to Madrid as soon as possible.

So Don and I found work. The Spanish account became a year-round effort for us. We visited every part of Spain as I made notes and Don took photos for reference (some of which were used in ads). I've checked my passport and found, much to my astonishment, that I was in Spain ten times during the eighteen months we worked on the business.

Now we needed something for Charlie.

Chivas Regal International came to sudden and surprising life with a request for a two-minute commercial to be run on intercontinental flights prior to the movie.

A commercial for booze? Something new in our lives! A two-minute spot? It seemed to give all the creative elbow room of a feature film. And best of all was the viewing environment, an airplane at movie time. That meant that our film would have to be entertainment, or run the risk of being resented.

Charlie and I had both done *New Yorker* cartoonist ads for Chivas over the years. What more natural than to take the best of these funny situations and lines and bring them to life, not as animation but as live-action film? We put a storyboard together and, with not much difficulty, sold the concept.

The number of actors alone sent us bidding out of the country. We wound up taking the low bid from a production company in Toronto.

Charlie spent almost three months in Toronto, with me sometimes and with Bob covering for me when I had to be in Spain or elsewhere. When we were finished, we had a good, funny film that exactly embodied the slightly smart-ass tone of two decades of Chivas magazine ads.

Everybody at Seagram loved it and could hardly wait to show it to the newly appointed head man of their division, a cigar-chomping salesman who liked to tell dirty jokes about minorities.

He hated the spot. Of course.

After viewing it twice, he said to his Marketing Director, "You see to it that these DDB guys never do another commecial for us. DDB doesn't know how to do commercials."

It ran anyway, as we had bought the time on the flights, and Seagram owned nothing else they could run. It never mattered that Chivas got fan mail about the spot. It never mattered that it won some nice awards. The official word at Seagram was that the film was a stinker.

What the hell. It had kept Charlie busy for a long time.

The next job for the two of us was a request from our Brussels office to come up with a campaign for a new business pitch. The client was a Belgium-based hamburger chain with outlets in five European countries. We won the account with an outrageous campaign that pretended that Ronald Reagan was in a state of mounting anxiety over the chance of a "Burger Gap" in Europe, as Quick (our new client) was catching up with American burger chains.

I went to Milan for a bitter cold and wet week in January to create a new business pitch and to gather background for another. At home again, I worked on it with Charlie.

Don and I spent February in Spain.

Then we went to Taiwan to get the briefing for a pitch to the late Chiang Kai-shek's ex-generals who were running China Airlines. It was an abstract adventure. China Airlines lived in a never-never land together with every other agency of the government of Taiwan.

First fantasy: there is no such place as Taiwan.

In their minds, *they* are the Republic of China. Those guys on the mainland are the People's Republic of China, so it was no use telling them that they were creating confusion by calling themselves China Airlines instead of Air Taiwan.

Our associates from the Hong Kong office, who had asked us into this party, told us to just forget it, and, in effect, shut up and pay attention to the meeting. Very politely, of course. Then they surprised us by presenting a complete campaign to the Taiwanese affiliate agency and the China Airlines point men.

The campaign was based on a Chinese belief in complete predestination, which somehow (and the logic still escapes me) leads them to the conviction that every moment should be seen as deserving of special attention.

Sure enough, their slogan was "We cherish each encounter."

We told them this wasn't going to work in Europe and the States, where the campaign was to run. It would be seen as over-promise, at least. We also tend to use the word *encounter* almost exclusively in a sexual context.

"Ah, so," they said.

We told them we would go back home and do a campaign that would deal with the home port origin of China Airlines without messing around with political convictions.

"Ah, so," they said.

After a week of the best Chinese food in our experience, we flew home and created a campaign. Don used the techniques of the traditional scroll paintings we had seen in the museum in Taipei, but in a fresh way that depicted contemporary life: airplanes, a stew serving drinks, a mechanic working on an aircraft engine.

Our slogan was "From Taipei to the World."

Taipei does exist, we had learned, even if Taiwan does not.

We sent it to DDB Hong Kong. Our people there suppressed it and presented only "We cherish each encounter."

The China Airlines generals bought *cherish*.

Second fantasy: You can overcome the Not-Invented-Here Factor.

The big surprise came from the least expected quarter.

Bob Levenson got Charlie, Don, and me together to tell us that he had decided to leave DDB. This was almost unthinkable news. Bob had been at the agency for twenty-six years and in the minds of most DDB's employees was the one person who most embodied the ideals and convictions of Bill Bernbach.

He didn't talk about why he was leaving, only about what he was going to do. He had agreed to join Saatchi & Saatchi Compton as Chief Creative Officer.

Compton? It was the dullest, dreariest old dog of an agency in the business, built on a close association with Procter & Gamble that went back some eighty years. What possible creative challenges could be offered by Tide, Ivory, Comet, Crisco, or Duncan Hines? Or by Johnson & Johnson's products such as Tylenol in all its forms? What had Bob done?

He had, he told us, flown to London a few weeks earlier at the urging of Ed Wax, Saatchi & Saatchi Compton's CEO, to meet with the elusive Charles and Maurice Saatchi. They had convinced him that they wanted S&S Compton, which they had acquired a couple of years earlier, to become a hot creative agency like their own London shop. It was the U.S. flagship of their growing worldwide empire, and they wanted it to be a showcase for Saatchi creativity.

They promised him their complete backing to make it happen, if not with current clients then with all the new business they knew that he and they could attract.

Bob wanted us to come with him.

It looked like a great adventure, a chance to do work that everyone would have their eyes on, work that might turn dull, plodding old Compton into a bright new agency.

It also looked like a job that needed doing, where poor, sad Doyle Dane Bernbach appeared to be in its death throes. (The agency had at last lost Polaroid, keeping only the International part of the business. I mentioned this just in case you have a taste for irony.) Our division was not really needed, and John Bernbach, who had just joined our group as president of DDB International, showed no signs of wanting to keep a creative group to do what we had been doing.

So we agreed to go with Bob to Saatchi.

Bob started on April 1. Don and I had a prior commitment to tour western and northern Spain for the entire month of May, together with our wives. We would also need June to turn the tour into the next campaign pitch for Spanish Tourism, an account that came up for competitive review on an annual basis.

While in Spain, we learned that Charlie had decided to start at Saatchi on the first of June. I started when the ads were done, on July 1. Don had some things to complete and wouldn't join us until fall.

The International job was finished after two years of paid vacations. We knew it had been too good to last.

LAST AGENCY BEFORE THE TURNPIKE

The agency business itself had been too good to last.

At least the agency business that I had known during its best years in New York had been too good to last. So it didn't last in New York. It got out of town.

Wonderful advertising was being made in Minneapolis, Boston, San Francisco, Atlanta, Dallas, and even more unlikely places.

Bright and eager young people were still starting their careers with confidence that advertising would be the one best place to find themselves, find their individual voices, make some difference in the world.

From Düsseldorf came a letter from a young friend, the son of a friend of mine from the early 60s. He was a German kid with the unlikely name of Oliver Grenville, and he was writing to tell me how things were doing in his first agency job.

Here are a few extracts from his letter:

> Well, David, maybe you can give me some advice on how to get an individual style, but I'm afraid there is no medicine to take, no pill that makes you a flexible, reliable copywriter. I'm sure I'll make it.
>
> Work is a lot of fun. So far I've written a whole campaign for computers. They all liked it a lot and made me lots of compliments. The client sent my copy back; he did not like it. Now I've written it all over again. I don't like it any longer—it seems stiff as hell. But the client loves it, raving how brilliant it is. Humor seems to be forbidden in this country. I also wrote about a very

healthy margarine, a sunflower oil, an airline, cheap champagne, and a new beer. One more in a market that contains more than 6,000 beers. All in all it's great. A lot of hard work, a lot of reading, and also learning to get tough.

I will continue to work at finding my style. The style that makes me a copywriter as good as David Herzbrun one day, or even as good as Oliver Grenville which might suit me even more.

The letter from Oliver sounded familiar in tone. It was my own voice, with a slight foreign accent, echoing back from thirty years ago; the voice of cocky confidence denying the existence of inconvenient realities.

And in New York, in the crumbling ruin of Compton, Charlie and I were still denying inconvenient realities by occasionally (almost covertly) creating good advertising. We did a couple of ads for British Airways that attracted a lot of notice in the trade press and won us some handsome awards in a few of the more prestigious shows.

Then London found out what we were doing, and we were ordered to stop it and only run adaptations of ads that had been created in London.

Okay, fair enough. We were a branch office. We quickly got a better understanding of how the DDB offices had felt when we would visit and show them their new Polaroid or Atari campaign.

I was about to start telling stories of our attempts to make fresh, intelligent, relevant, smart advertising for Procter & Gamble, Johnson & Johnson, American Home Products, and other inflexible old Compton accounts. I was actually forming a sentence when I told myself to stop. There is no good reason to put myself, much less you, through a dozen dreary pages before bringing this memoir to an end.

I'll give it to you in broad strokes.

There I was, as I had been before, at the center of what was presumed to be The Action. The trade press was full of the Saatchi brothers, speculating on their plans, wondering at their acquisitions and their acquisitiveness. Omnicom's Mega-Merger was countered with a humongomerger when the Saatchis bought Ted Bates as the ad world wondered. The buy of the giant Bates made them the world's biggest advertising company. All of my friends asked me what the hell was going on. "You may well ask," was my usual reply.

The wind was certainly blowing, and it was certainly hell, but as you know, in the center of the hurricane it is eerily calm. At sad old (Saatchi & Saatchi) Compton, there was not a breath of air, no hint of a breeze. We drifted, rudderless, in an oily swell beneath a threatening sky. My early hopes, as a born-again realist, were limited. My banner was surely a hedged bet. I had hung on my office wall a London street sign from Old Compton Street and had crossed out the *Old* and inserted, over a caret, the phrase, *NEW, IMPROVED*. I had thought we could deliver on that much, but in fact I was wrong.

Most Compton clients were happy with Compton ways. They had little interest in Saatchi & Saatchi and none in transplanted creatives from the old DDB. And so we beat on, boats against the current.

When the Saatchis bought Ted Bates, they destroyed any image they might have had of being interested in creative agencies. The Bates buy also cost Compton some $60 million in lost Procter business, due to P&G's perception of conflicts with business in other Saatchi agencies.

When Procter bailed out, other clients got nervous and followed suit. We needed new business desperately, but we, as the only U.S. agency to carry the Saatchi name, suddenly became untouchable. Nobody wanted to talk to us.

In order to meet the cash contributions required by the parent company, we had to fire a great many people.

The atmosphere in the agency, which had been stale when we arrived, deteriorated to fetid. The morale sank, whimpering, to the floor.

It was a time when vital leadership was needed. Ed Wax, while a decent man and a fine account manager, just didn't have the dynamism and presence to be a leader, to inspirit the staff. Nor did he have the sales ability to counter, or even try to counter, the growing uncertainty that clients and prospects felt about the Saatchi brothers.

Suddenly there were no more meetings of the board of directors. I did not see Ed for weeks at a time, and I suspected that he was holed up in his office, waiting for the wind to stop blowing.

One of my friends at another agency called and asked what was gong on. "I assumed," he said, "that when Levenson and you went to Compton, the place would take off and fly."

"Right," I said. "Fly. In fact it *is* a lot like the Icarus myth."

"How so?" he asked.

"It's got the same moral," I said. "Don't put too much confidence in Wax "

One by one, most of my accounts found new agencies. My writers and art directors drifted in and out of my office in vain hopes of finding something to do, or at least finding out what was going on. I didn't know what was going on, but they didn't quite believe me when I told them. I was an Executive V.P., wasn't I? And a member of the board of directors?

Sure I was. But the real board of directors sat in London, where the real decisions were made.

They were made by people who owned us but who never once bothered to visit us, or even to send a staff memo or a fake but cheery newsletter. The brothers were so insensitive to their American employees that they ran a two-page ad in the *New York Times*, only days after we had been forced into drastic staff cuts, telling the financial community how well the parent company was doing, how gross revenues and net income had dramatically increased, and how rosy the future appeared when viewed from London.

They failed to understand when our PR director cancelled distribution to the staff of preprints of the ad. They thought it would be good for our morale to learn how well "our" company was doing.

It was appalling. And I was appalled.

When I had come to Saatchi & Saatchi Compton, it was with a plan to work for only three years and then see if I could retire. After only a year and a half of this sad, moribund place I decided to shorten the timetable. I told Bob that I would retire in six months.

In my last four months, therefore, I had nothing whatever to work on. All that was left for me in the agency business was the memory of some wonderful people, interesting times and places, funny stories, good stories, war stories, and horror stories.

So I started writing this book.

I announced my retirement officially in May. I left at the end of June to start a new life, to finish this book, and to write others. To do some consulting and create some advertising too. For a very few clients I like.

Patch gave a dinner party to celebrate my retirement. The guest list looked like an index to this book, or pages from *Who's Who in Advertising*. It was a great party, and we all had a lot of laughs.

Lord, it was good to laugh again.